Elastic Load Balancing Application Load Balancers

A catalogue record for this book is available from the Hong Kong Public Libraries.

Published in Hong Kong by Samurai Media Limited.

Email: info@samuraimedia.org

ISBN 9789888408092

Contents

What Is an Application Load Balancer?

Elastic Load Balancing supports three types of load balancers: Application Load Balancers, Network Load Balancers, and Classic Load Balancers. This guide discusses Application Load Balancers. For more information about Network Load Balancers, see the User Guide for Network Load Balancers. For more information about Classic Load Balancers, see the User Guide for Classic Load Balancers.

Application Load Balancer Components

A *load balancer* serves as the single point of contact for clients. The load balancer distributes incoming application traffic across multiple targets, such as EC2 instances, in multiple Availability Zones. This increases the availability of your application. You add one or more listeners to your load balancer.

A *listener* checks for connection requests from clients, using the protocol and port that you configure, and forwards requests to one or more target groups, based on the rules that you define. Each rule specifies a target group, condition, and priority. When the condition is met, the traffic is forwarded to the target group. You must define a default rule for each listener, and you can add rules that specify different target groups based on the content of the request (also known as *content-based routing*).

Each *target group* routes requests to one or more registered targets, such as EC2 instances, using the protocol and port number that you specify. You can register a target with multiple target groups. You can configure health checks on a per target group basis. Health checks are performed on all targets registered to a target group that is specified in a listener rule for your load balancer.

The following diagram illustrates the basic components. Notice that each listener contains a default rule, and one listener contains another rule that routes requests to a different target group. One target is registered with two target groups.

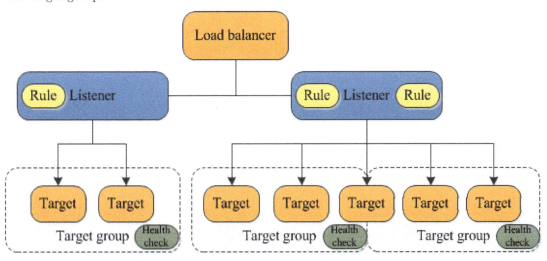

For more information, see the following documentation:

- Load Balancers
- Listeners
- Target Groups

Application Load Balancer Overview

An Application Load Balancer functions at the application layer, the seventh layer of the Open Systems Interconnection (OSI) model. After the load balancer receives a request, it evaluates the listener rules in priority order to determine which rule to apply, and then selects a target from the target group for the rule action using the round robin routing algorithm. Note that you can configure listener rules to route requests to different target groups based on the content of the application traffic. Routing is performed independently for each target group, even when a target is registered with multiple target groups.

You can add and remove targets from your load balancer as your needs change, without disrupting the overall flow of requests to your application. Elastic Load Balancing scales your load balancer as traffic to your application changes over time. Elastic Load Balancing can scale to the vast majority of workloads automatically.

You can configure health checks, which are used to monitor the health of the registered targets so that the load balancer can send requests only to the healthy targets.

For more information, see How Elastic Load Balancing Works in the *Elastic Load Balancing User Guide*.

Benefits of Migrating from a Classic Load Balancer

Using an Application Load Balancer instead of a Classic Load Balancer has the following benefits:

- Support for path-based routing. You can configure rules for your listener that forward requests based on the URL in the request. This enables you to structure your application as smaller services, and route requests to the correct service based on the content of the URL.
- Support for host-based routing. You can configure rules for your listener that forward requests based on the host field in the HTTP header. This enables you to route requests to multiple domains using a single load balancer.
- Support for routing requests to multiple applications on a single EC2 instance. You can register each instance or IP address with the same target group using multiple ports.
- Support for registering targets by IP address, including targets outside the VPC for the load balancer.
- Support for containerized applications. Amazon Elastic Container Service (Amazon ECS) can select an unused port when scheduling a task and register the task with a target group using this port. This enables you to make efficient use of your clusters.
- Support for monitoring the health of each service independently, as health checks are defined at the target group level and many CloudWatch metrics are reported at the target group level. Attaching a target group to an Auto Scaling group enables you to scale each service dynamically based on demand.
- Access logs contain additional information and are stored in compressed format.
- Improved load balancer performance.

For more information about the features supported by each load balancer type, see Comparison of Elastic Load Balancing Products.

How to Get Started

To create an Application Load Balancer, try one of the following tutorials:

- Getting Started with Elastic Load Balancing in the *Elastic Load Balancing User Guide*.
- Tutorial: Use Path-Based Routing with Your Application Load Balancer
- Tutorial: Use Microservices as Targets with Your Application Load Balancer

Pricing

With your load balancer, you pay only for what you use. For more information, see Elastic Load Balancing Pricing.

Getting Started with Application Load Balancers

This tutorial provides a hands-on introduction to Application Load Balancers through the AWS Management Console, a web-based interface. To create your first Application Load Balancer, complete the following steps.

Topics

- Before You Begin
- Step 1: Select a Load Balancer Type
- Step 2: Configure Your Load Balancer and Listener
- Step 3: Configure a Security Group for Your Load Balancer
- Step 4: Configure Your Target Group
- Step 5: Register Targets with Your Target Group
- Step 6: Create and Test Your Load Balancer
- Step 7: Delete Your Load Balancer (Optional)

Alternatively, to create a Network Load Balancer, see Getting Started with Network Load Balancers in the *User Guide for Network Load Balancers*. To create a Classic Load Balancer, see Create a Classic Load Balancer in the *User Guide for Classic Load Balancers*.

Before You Begin

- Decide which two Availability Zones you will use for your EC2 instances. Configure your virtual private cloud (VPC) with at least one public subnet in each of these Availability Zones. These public subnets are used to configure the load balancer. You can launch your EC2 instances in other subnets of these Availability Zones instead.
- Launch at least one EC2 instance in each Availability Zone. Be sure to install a web server, such as Apache or Internet Information Services (IIS), on each EC2 instance. Ensure that the security groups for these instances allow HTTP access on port 80.

Step 1: Select a Load Balancer Type

Elastic Load Balancing supports three types of load balancers. For this tutorial, you create an Application Load Balancer.

To create an Application Load Balancer

1. Open the Amazon EC2 console at https://console.aws.amazon.com/ec2/.

2. On the navigation bar, choose a region for your load balancer. Be sure to select the same region that you used for your EC2 instances.

3. On the navigation pane, under **LOAD BALANCING**, choose **Load Balancers**.

4. Choose **Create Load Balancer**.

5. For **Application Load Balancer**, choose **Create**.

Step 2: Configure Your Load Balancer and Listener

On the **Configure Load Balancer** page, complete the following procedure.

To configure your load balancer and listener

1. For **Name**, type a name for your load balancer.

The name of your Application Load Balancer must be unique within your set of Application Load Balancers and Network Load Balancers for the region, can have a maximum of 32 characters, can contain only alphanumeric characters and hyphens, must not begin or end with a hyphen, and must not begin with "internal-".

2. For **Scheme** and **IP address type**, keep the default values.

3. For **Listeners**, keep the default, which is a listener that accepts HTTP traffic on port 80.

4. For **Availability Zones**, select the VPC that you used for your EC2 instances. For each Availability Zone that you used to launch your EC2 instances, select the Availability Zone and then select the public subnet for that Availability Zone.

5. Choose **Next: Configure Security Settings**.

6. For this tutorial, you are not creating an HTTPS listener. Choose **Next: Configure Security Groups**.

Step 3: Configure a Security Group for Your Load Balancer

The security group for your load balancer must allow it to communicate with registered targets on both the listener port and the health check port. The console can create a security group for your load balancer on your behalf, with rules that specify the correct protocols and ports. If you prefer, you can create and select your own security group instead. For more information, see Recommended Rules.

On the **Configure Security Groups** page, complete the following procedure to have Elastic Load Balancing create a security group for your load balancer on your behalf.

To configure a security group for your load balancer

1. Choose **Create a new security group**.

2. Type a name and description for the security group, or keep the default name and description. This new security group contains a rule that allows traffic to the load balancer listener port that you selected on the **Configure Load Balancer** page.

3. Choose **Next: Configure Routing**.

Step 4: Configure Your Target Group

Create a target group, which is used in request routing. The default rule for your listener routes requests to the registered targets in this target group. The load balancer checks the health of targets in this target group using the health check settings defined for the target group. On the **Configure Routing** page, complete the following procedure.

To configure your target group

1. For **Target group**, keep the default, **New target group**.

2. For **Name**, type a name for the new target group.

3. Keep **Protocol** as HTTP, **Port** as 80, and **Target type** as instance.

4. For **Health checks**, keep the default protocol and ping path.

5. Choose **Next: Register Targets**.

Step 5: Register Targets with Your Target Group

On the **Register Targets** page, complete the following procedure.

To register targets with the target group

1. For **Instances**, select one or more instances.

2. Keep the default port, 80, and choose **Add to registered**.

3. When you have finished selecting instances, choose **Next: Review**.

Step 6: Create and Test Your Load Balancer

Before creating the load balancer, review the settings that you selected. After creating the load balancer, verify that it's sending traffic to your EC2 instances.

To create and test your load balancer

1. On the **Review** page, choose **Create**.

2. After you are notified that your load balancer was created successfully, choose **Close**.

3. On the navigation pane, under **LOAD BALANCING**, choose **Target Groups**.

4. Select the newly created target group.

5. On the **Targets** tab, verify that your instances are ready. If the status of an instance is `initial`, it's probably because the instance is still in the process of being registered, or it has not passed the minimum number of health checks to be considered healthy. After the status of at least one instance is `healthy`, you can test your load balancer.

6. On the navigation pane, under **LOAD BALANCING**, choose **Load Balancers**.

7. Select the newly created load balancer.

8. On the **Description** tab, copy the DNS name of the load balancer (for example, my-load-balancer-1234567890.us-west-2.elb.amazonaws.com). Paste the DNS name into the address field of an Internet-connected web browser. If everything is working, the browser displays the default page of your server.

9. (Optional) To define additional listener rules, see Add a Rule.

Step 7: Delete Your Load Balancer (Optional)

As soon as your load balancer becomes available, you are billed for each hour or partial hour that you keep it running. When you no longer need a load balancer, you can delete it. As soon as the load balancer is deleted, you stop incurring charges for it. Note that deleting a load balancer does not affect the targets registered with the load balancer. For example, your EC2 instances continue to run.

To delete your load balancer

1. Open the Amazon EC2 console at https://console.aws.amazon.com/ec2/.

2. On the navigation pane, under **LOAD BALANCING**, choose **Load Balancers**.

3. Select the checkbox for the load balancer, and then choose **Actions, Delete**.

4. When prompted for confirmation, choose **Yes, Delete**.

Tutorials for Application Load Balancers

The following Elastic Load Balancing tutorials show you how to perform common tasks using an Application Load Balancer.

- Getting Started with Elastic Load Balancing (*Elastic Load Balancing User Guide*)
- Tutorial: Use Path-Based Routing with Your Application Load Balancer
- Tutorial: Use Microservices as Targets with Your Application Load Balancer
- Tutorial: Create an Application Load Balancer Using the AWS CLI

Tutorial: Use Path-Based Routing with Your Application Load Balancer

You can create a listener with rules to forward requests based on the URL path. This is known as *path-based routing*. If you are running microservices, you can route traffic to multiple back-end services using path-based routing. For example, you can route general requests to one target group and requests to render images to another target group.

Before You Begin

- Launch your EC2 instances in a virtual private cloud (VPC). Ensure that the security groups for these instances allow access on the listener port and the health check port. For more information, see Target Security Groups.
- Verify that your microservices are deployed on the EC2 instances that you plan to register.

Create Your Load Balancer

To create a load balancer that uses path-based routing

1. Open the Amazon EC2 console at https://console.aws.amazon.com/ec2/.

2. On the navigation bar, select the same region that you selected for your EC2 instances.

3. On the navigation pane, under **LOAD BALANCING**, choose **Target Groups**.

4. Create a target group for the first set of targets as follows:

   1. Choose **Create target group**.

   2. Specify a name, protocol, port, and VPC for the target group, and then choose **Create**.

   3. Select the new target group.

   4. On the **Targets** tab, choose **Edit**.

   5. For **Instances**, select one or more instances. Specify a port for the instances, choose **Add to registered**, and then choose **Save**.

      Note that the status of the instances is `initial` until the instances are registered and have passed health checks, and then it is `unused` until you configure the target group to receive traffic from the load balancer.

5. Create a target group for the second set of targets as follows:

   1. Choose **Create target group**.

   2. Specify a name, protocol, port, and VPC for the target group, and then choose **Create**.

   3. On the **Targets** tab, choose **Edit**.

   4. For **Instances**, select one or more instances. Specify a port for the instances, choose **Add to registered**, and then choose **Save**.

      Note that the status of the instances is `initial` until the instances are registered and have passed health checks, and then it is `unused` until you configure the target group to receive traffic from the load balancer.

6. On the navigation pane, under **LOAD BALANCING**, choose **Load Balancers**.

7. Choose **Create Load Balancer**.

8. For **Select load balancer type**, choose **Application Load Balancer**.

9. Choose **Continue**.

10. Complete the **Configure Load Balancer** page as follows:

    1. For **Name**, type a name for your load balancer.

       The name of your Application Load Balancer must be unique within your set of Application Load Balancers and Network Load Balancers for the region, can have a maximum of 32 characters, can contain only alphanumeric characters and hyphens, and must not begin or end with a hyphen.

    2. For **Scheme**, an Internet-facing load balancer routes requests from clients over the Internet to targets. An internal load balancer routes requests to targets using private IP addresses.

    3. For **Listeners**, the default is a listener that accepts HTTP traffic on port 80. You can keep the default listener settings, modify the protocol or port of the listener, or choose **Add** to add another listener.

    4. For **Availability Zones**, select the VPC that you used for your EC2 instances. Select at least two Availability Zones. If there is one subnet for an Availability Zone, it is selected. If there is more than one subnet for an Availability Zone, select one of the subnets. Note that you can select only one subnet per Availability Zone.

    5. Choose **Next: Configure Security Settings**.

11. (Optional) If you created a secure listener in the previous step, complete the **Configure Security Settings** page as follows:

    1. If you created or imported a certificate using AWS Certificate Manager, select **Choose an existing certificate from AWS Certificate Manager (ACM)**, and then select the certificate from **Certificate name**.

    2. If you uploaded a certificate using IAM, select **Choose an existing certificate from AWS Identity and Access Management (IAM)**, and then select your certificate from **Certificate name**.

    3. If you have a certificate to upload but ACM is not supported in your region, choose **Upload a new SSL Certificate to AWS Identity and Access Management (IAM)**. For **Certificate name**, type a name for the certificate. For **Private Key**, copy and paste the contents of the private key file (PEM-encoded). In **Public Key Certificate**, copy and paste the contents of the public key certificate file (PEM-encoded). In **Certificate Chain**, copy and paste the contents of the certificate chain file (PEM-encoded), unless you are using a self-signed certificate and it's not important that browsers implicitly accept the certificate.

    4. For **Select policy**, keep the default security policy.

12. Choose **Next: Configure Security Groups**.

13. Complete the **Configure Security Groups** page as follows:

    1. Select **Create a new security group**.

    2. Type a name and description for the security group, or keep the default name and description. This new security group contains a rule that allows traffic to the port that you selected for your load balancer on the **Configure Load Balancer** page.

    3. Choose **Next: Configure Routing**.

14. Complete the **Configure Routing** page as follows:

    1. For **Target group**, choose `Existing target group`.

    2. For **Name**, choose the first target group that you created.

    3. Choose **Next: Register Targets**.

15. On the **Register Targets** page, the instances that you registered with the target group appear under **Registered instances**. You can't modify the targets registered with the target group until after you complete the wizard. Choose **Next: Review**.

16. On the **Review** page, choose **Create**.

17. After you are notified that your load balancer was created successfully, choose **Close**.

18. Select the newly created load balancer.

19. On the **Listeners** tab, use the arrow to view the rules for the listener, and then choose **Add rule**. Specify the rule as follows:

    1. For **Target group name**, choose the second target group that you created.

    2. For **Path pattern** specify the exact pattern to be used for path-based routing (for example, /img/*). For more information, see Listener Rules.

    3. Choose **Save**.

Tutorial: Use Microservices as Targets with Your Application Load Balancer

You can use a microservices architecture to structure your application as services that you can develop and deploy independently. You can install one or more of these services on each EC2 instance, with each service accepting connections on a different port. You can use a single Application Load Balancer to route requests to all the services for your application. When you register an EC2 instance with a target group, you can register it multiple times; for each service, register the instance using the port for the service.

Important
When you deploy your services using Amazon Elastic Container Service (Amazon ECS), you can use dynamic port mapping to support multiple tasks from a single service on the same container instance. Amazon ECS manages updates to your services by automatically registering and deregistering containers with your target group using the instance ID and port for each container. For more information, see Service Load Balancing in the *Amazon Elastic Container Service Developer Guide*.

Before You Begin

- Launch your EC2 instances. Ensure that the security groups for the instances allow access from the load balancer security group on the listener ports and the health check ports. For more information, see Target Security Groups.
- Deploy your services to your EC2 instances (for example, using containers.)

Create Your Load Balancer

To create a load balancer that uses multiple services as targets

1. Open the Amazon EC2 console at https://console.aws.amazon.com/ec2/.

2. On the navigation bar, select the same region that you selected for your EC2 instances.

3. On the navigation pane, under **LOAD BALANCING**, choose **Load Balancers**.

4. Choose **Create Load Balancer**.

5. For **Select load balancer type**, choose **Application Load Balancer**.

6. Choose **Continue**.

7. Complete the **Configure Load Balancer** page as follows:

   1. For **Name**, type a name for your load balancer.

      The name of your Application Load Balancer must be unique within your set of Application Load Balancers and Network Load Balancers for the region, can have a maximum of 32 characters, can contain only alphanumeric characters and hyphens, and must not begin or end with a hyphen.

   2. For **Scheme**, an Internet-facing load balancer routes requests from clients over the Internet to targets. An internal load balancer routes requests to targets using private IP addresses.

   3. For **Listeners**, the default is a listener that accepts HTTP traffic on port 80. You can keep the default listener settings, modify the protocol or port of the listener, or choose **Add** to add another listener.

   4. For **Availability Zones**, select the VPC that you used for your EC2 instances. Select at least two Availability Zones. If there is one subnet for an Availability Zone, it is selected. If there is more than one subnet for an Availability Zone, select one of the subnets. Note that you can select only one subnet per Availability Zone.

16

5. Choose **Next: Configure Security Settings**.

8. (Optional) If you created a secure listener in the previous step, complete the **Configure Security Settings** page as follows:

    1. If you created or imported a certificate using AWS Certificate Manager, select **Choose an existing certificate from AWS Certificate Manager (ACM)**, and then select the certificate from **Certificate name**.

    2. If you uploaded a certificate using IAM, select **Choose an existing certificate from AWS Identity and Access Management (IAM)**, and then select the certificate from **Certificate name**.

    3. If you have a certificate to upload but ACM is not supported in your region, choose **Upload a new SSL Certificate to AWS Identity and Access Management (IAM)**. For **Certificate name**, type a name for the certificate. For **Private Key**, copy and paste the contents of the private key file (PEM-encoded). In **Public Key Certificate**, copy and paste the contents of the public key certificate file (PEM-encoded). In **Certificate Chain**, copy and paste the contents of the certificate chain file (PEM-encoded), unless you are using a self-signed certificate and it's not important that browsers implicitly accept the certificate.

    4. For **Select policy**, keep the default security policy.

9. Choose **Next: Configure Security Groups**.

10. Complete the **Configure Security Groups** page as follows:

    1. Select **Create a new security group**.

    2. Type a name and description for the security group, or keep the default name and description. This new security group contains a rule that allows traffic to the port that you selected for your load balancer on the **Configure Load Balancer** page.

    3. Choose **Next: Configure Routing**.

11. Complete the **Configure Routing** page as follows:

    1. For **Target group**, keep the default, `New target group`.

    2. For **Name**, type a name for the new target group.

    3. Set **Protocol** and **Port** as needed.

    4. For **Health checks**, keep the default health check settings.

    5. Choose **Next: Register Targets**.

12. For **Register Targets**, do the following:

    1. For **Instances**, select an EC2 instance.

    2. Type the port used by the service, and then choose **Add to registered**.

    3. Repeat for each service to register. When you are finished, choose **Next: Review**.

13. On the **Review** page, choose **Create**.

14. After you are notified that your load balancer was created successfully, choose **Close**.

Tutorial: Create an Application Load Balancer Using the AWS CLI

This tutorial provides a hands-on introduction to Application Load Balancers through the AWS CLI.

Before You Begin

- Use the following command to verify that you are running a version of the AWS CLI that supports Application Load Balancers.

```
1 aws elbv2 help
```

   If you get an error message that elbv2 is not a valid choice, update your AWS CLI. For more information, see Installing the AWS Command Line Interface in the *AWS Command Line Interface User Guide*.

- Launch your EC2 instances in a virtual private cloud (VPC). Ensure that the security groups for these instances allow access on the listener port and the health check port. For more information, see Target Security Groups.

Create Your Load Balancer

To create your first load balancer, complete the following steps.

To create a load balancer

1. Use the create-load-balancer command to create a load balancer. You must specify two subnets that are not from the same Availability Zone.

```
1 aws elbv2 create-load-balancer --name my-load-balancer  \
2 --subnets subnet-12345678 subnet-23456789 --security-groups sg-12345678
```

   The output includes the Amazon Resource Name (ARN) of the load balancer, with the following format:

```
1 arn:aws:elasticloadbalancing:us-east-2:123456789012:loadbalancer/app/my-load-balancer
     /1234567890123456
```

2. Use the create-target-group command to create a target group, specifying the same VPC that you used for your EC2 instances:

```
1 aws elbv2 create-target-group --name my-targets --protocol HTTP --port 80 \
2 --vpc-id vpc-12345678
```

   The output includes the ARN of the target group, with this format:

```
1 arn:aws:elasticloadbalancing:us-east-2:123456789012:targetgroup/my-targets/1234567890123456
```

3. Use the register-targets command to register your instances with your target group:

```
1 aws elbv2 register-targets --target-group-arn targetgroup-arn  \
2 --targets Id=i-12345678 Id=i-23456789
```

4. Use the create-listener command to create a listener for your load balancer with a default rule that forwards requests to your target group:

```
1 aws elbv2 create-listener --load-balancer-arn loadbalancer-arn \
2 --protocol HTTP --port 80  \
3 --default-actions Type=forward,TargetGroupArn=targetgroup-arn
```

   The output contains the ARN of the listener, with the following format:

```
1  arn:aws:elasticloadbalancing:us-east-2:123456789012:listener/app/my-load-balancer
     /1234567890123456/1234567890123456
```

5. (Optional) You can verify the health of the registered targets for your target group using this describe-target-health command:

```
1  aws elbv2 describe-target-health --target-group-arn targetgroup-arn
```

Add an HTTPS Listener

If you have a load balancer with an HTTP listener, you can add an HTTPS listener as follows.

To add an HTTPS listener to your load balancer

1. Create an SSL certificate for use with your load balancer using one of the following methods:

   - Create or import the certificate using AWS Certificate Manager (ACM). For more information, see Request a Certificate or Importing Certificates in the *AWS Certificate Manager User Guide*.
   - Upload the certificate using AWS Identity and Access Management (IAM). For more information, see Working with Server Certificates in the *IAM User Guide*.

2. Use the create-listener command to create the listener with a default rule that forwards requests to your target group. You must specify an SSL certificate when you create an HTTPS listener. Note that you can specify an SSL policy other than the default using the `--ssl-policy` option.

```
1  aws elbv2 create-listener --load-balancer-arn loadbalancer-arn \
2  --protocol HTTPS --port 443  \
3  --certificates CertificateArn=certificate-arn \
4  --default-actions Type=forward,TargetGroupArn=targetgroup-arn
```

Add Targets Using Port Overrides

If you have multiple ECS containers on a single instance, each container accepts connections on a different port. You can register the instance with the target group multiple times, each time with a different port.

To add targets using port overrides

1. Use the create-target-group command to create a target group:

```
1  aws elbv2 create-target-group --name my-targets --protocol HTTP --port 80 \
2  --vpc-id vpc-12345678
```

2. Use the register-targets command to register your instances with your target group. Notice that the instance IDs are the same for each container, but the ports are different.

```
1  aws elbv2 register-targets --target-group-arn targetgroup-arn  \
2  --targets Id=i-12345678,Port=80 Id=i-12345678,Port=766
```

3. Use the create-rule command to add a rule to your listener that forwards requests to the target group:

```
1  aws elbv2 create-rule --listener-arn listener-arn --priority 10 \
2  --actions Type=forward,TargetGroupArn=targetgroup-arn
```

Add Path-Based Routing

If you have a listener with a default rule that forwards requests to one target group, you can add a rule that forwards requests to another target group based on URL. For example, you can route general requests to one target group and requests to display images to another target group.

To add a rule to a listener with a path pattern

1. Use the create-target-group command to create a target group:

```
1 aws elbv2 create-target-group --name my-targets --protocol HTTP --port 80 \
2 --vpc-id vpc-12345678
```

2. Use the register-targets command to register your instances with your target group:

```
1 aws elbv2 register-targets --target-group-arn targetgroup-arn  \
2 --targets Id=i-12345678 Id=i-23456789
```

3. Use the create-rule command to add a rule to your listener that forwards requests to the target group if the URL contains the specified pattern:

```
1 aws elbv2 create-rule --listener-arn listener-arn --priority 10 \
2 --conditions Field=path-pattern,Values='/img/*' \
3 --actions Type=forward,TargetGroupArn=targetgroup-arn
```

Delete Your Load Balancer

When you no longer need your load balancer and target group, you can delete them as follows:

```
1 aws elbv2 delete-load-balancer --load-balancer-arn loadbalancer-arn
2 aws elbv2 delete-target-group --target-group-arn targetgroup-arn
```

Application Load Balancers

A *load balancer* serves as the single point of contact for clients. Clients send requests to the load balancer, and the load balancer sends them to targets, such as EC2 instances, in two or more Availability Zones. To configure your load balancer, you create target groups, and then register targets with your target groups. You also create listeners to check for connection requests from clients, and listener rules to route requests from clients to the targets in one or more target groups.

Topics

- Load Balancer Security Groups
- Load Balancer State
- Load Balancer Attributes
- IP Address Type
- Deletion Protection
- Connection Idle Timeout
- Application Load Balancers and AWS WAF
- Create a Load Balancer
- Update Availability Zones
- Update Security Groups
- Update the Address Type
- Update Tags
- Delete a Load Balancer

Load Balancer Security Groups

A *security group* acts as a firewall that controls the traffic allowed to and from your load balancer. You can choose the ports and protocols to allow for both inbound and outbound traffic.

The rules for the security groups associated with your load balancer security group must allow traffic in both directions on both the listener and the health check ports. Whenever you add a listener to a load balancer or update the health check port for a target group, you must review your security group rules to ensure that they allow traffic on the new port in both directions. For more information, see Recommended Rules.

Load Balancer State

A load balancer can be in one of the following states:

`provisioning`
The load balancer is being set up.

`active`
The load balancer is fully set up and ready to route traffic.

`failed`
The load balancer could not be set up.

Load Balancer Attributes

The following are the load balancer attributes:

`access_logs.s3.enabled`
Indicates whether access logs stored in Amazon S3 are enabled. The default is `false`.

`access_logs.s3.bucket`
The name of the S3 bucket for the access logs. This attribute is required if access logs are enabled. For more information, see Bucket Permissions.

`access_logs.s3.prefix`
The prefix for the location in the S3 bucket.

`deletion_protection.enabled`
Indicates whether deletion protection is enabled. The default is `false`.

`idle_timeout.timeout_seconds`
The idle timeout value, in seconds. The default is 60 seconds.

`routing.http2.enabled`
Indicates whether HTTP/2 is enabled. The default is `true`.

IP Address Type

You can set the IP address type of your Internet-facing load balancer when you create it or after it is active. Note that internal load balancers must use IPv4 addresses.

The following are the load balancer IP address types:

`ipv4`
The load balancer supports only IPv4 addresses (for example, 192.0.2.1)

`dualstack`
The load balancer supports both IPv4 and IPv6 addresses (for example, 2001:0db8:85a3:0:0:8a2e:0370:7334).

Clients that communicate with the load balancer using IPv4 addresses resolve the A record and clients that communicate with the load balancer using IPv6 addresses resolve the AAAA record. However, the load balancer communicates with its targets using IPv4 addresses, regardless of how the client communicates with the load balancer.

For more information, see IP Address Types for Your Application Load Balancer.

Deletion Protection

To prevent your load balancer from being deleted accidentally, you can enable deletion protection. By default, deletion protection is disabled for your load balancer.

If you enable deletion protection for your load balancer, you must disable it before you can delete the load balancer.

To enable deletion protection using the console

1. Open the Amazon EC2 console at https://console.aws.amazon.com/ec2/.

2. On the navigation pane, under **LOAD BALANCING**, choose **Load Balancers**.

3. Select the load balancer.

4. On the **Description** tab, choose **Edit attributes**.

5. On the **Edit load balancer attributes** page, select **Enable** for **Delete Protection**, and then choose **Save**.

6. Choose **Save**.

To disable deletion protection using the console

1. Open the Amazon EC2 console at https://console.aws.amazon.com/ec2/.

2. On the navigation pane, under **LOAD BALANCING**, choose **Load Balancers**.

3. Select the load balancer.

4. On the **Description** tab, choose **Edit attributes**.

5. On the **Edit load balancer attributes** page, clear **Enable** for **Delete Protection**, and then choose **Save**.

6. Choose **Save**.

To enable or disable deletion protection using the AWS CLI

Use the modify-load-balancer-attributes command with the `deletion_protection.enabled` attribute.

Connection Idle Timeout

For each request that a client makes through a load balancer, the load balancer maintains two connections. A front-end connection is between a client and the load balancer, and a back-end connection is between the load balancer and a target. For each front-end connection, the load balancer manages an idle timeout that is triggered when no data is sent over the connection for a specified time period. If no data has been sent or received by the time that the idle timeout period elapses, the load balancer closes the front-end connection.

By default, Elastic Load Balancing sets the idle timeout value to 60 seconds. Therefore, if the target doesn't send some data at least every 60 seconds while the request is in flight, the load balancer can close the front-end connection. To ensure that lengthy operations such as file uploads have time to complete, send at least 1 byte of data before each idle timeout period elapses, and increase the length of the idle timeout period as needed.

For back-end connections, we recommend that you enable the HTTP keep-alive option for your EC2 instances. You can enable HTTP keep-alive in the web server settings for your EC2 instances. If you enable HTTP keep-alive, the load balancer can reuse back-end connections until the keep-alive timeout expires.

To update the idle timeout value using the console

1. Open the Amazon EC2 console at https://console.aws.amazon.com/ec2/.

2. On the navigation pane, under **LOAD BALANCING**, choose **Load Balancers**.

3. Select the load balancer.

4. On the **Description** tab, choose **Edit attributes**.

5. On the **Edit load balancer attributes** page, type a value for **Idle timeout**, in seconds. The valid range is 1-4000. The default is 60 seconds.

6. Choose **Save**.

To update the idle timeout value using the AWS CLI

Use the modify-load-balancer-attributes command with the `idle_timeout.timeout_seconds` attribute.

Application Load Balancers and AWS WAF

You can use AWS WAF with your Application Load Balancer to allow or block requests based on the rules in a web access control list (web ACL). For more information, see Working with Web ACLs in the *AWS WAF Developer Guide*.

Create an Application Load Balancer

A load balancer takes requests from clients and distributes them across targets in a target group.

Before you begin, ensure that you have a virtual private cloud (VPC) with at least one public subnet in each of the Availability Zones used by your targets.

To create a load balancer using the AWS CLI, see Tutorial: Create an Application Load Balancer Using the AWS CLI.

To create a load balancer using the AWS Management Console, complete the following tasks.

Topics

- Step 1: Configure a Load Balancer and a Listener
- Step 2: Configure Security Settings for an HTTPS Listener
- Step 3: Configure a Security Group
- Step 4: Configure a Target Group
- Step 5: Configure Targets for the Target Group
- Step 6: Create the Load Balancer

Step 1: Configure a Load Balancer and a Listener

First, provide some basic configuration information for your load balancer, such as a name, a network, and one or more listeners. A listener is a process that checks for connection requests. It is configured with a protocol and a port for connections from clients to the load balancer. For more information about supported protocols and ports, see Listener Configuration.

To configure your load balancer and listener

1. Open the Amazon EC2 console at https://console.aws.amazon.com/ec2/.

2. On the navigation pane, under **LOAD BALANCING**, choose **Load Balancers**.

3. Choose **Create Load Balancer**.

4. For **Application Load Balancer**, choose **Create**.

5. For **Name**, type a name for your load balancer. For example, **my-alb**.

6. For **Scheme**, an Internet-facing load balancer routes requests from clients over the Internet to targets. An internal load balancer routes requests to targets using private IP addresses.

7. For **Listeners**, the default is a listener that accepts HTTP traffic on port 80. You can keep the default listener settings, modify the protocol, or modify the port. Choose **Add** to add another listener (for example, an HTTPS listener).

8. For **Availability Zones**, select at least two Availability Zones from your VPC. If there is one subnet for an Availability Zone, it is selected. If there is more than one subnet for an Availability Zone, select one of the subnets. Note that you can select only one subnet per Availability Zone.

9. Choose **Next: Configure Security Settings**.

Step 2: Configure Security Settings for an HTTPS Listener

If you created an HTTPS listener in the previous step, configure the required security settings. Otherwise, go to the next page in the wizard.

When you use HTTPS for your load balancer listener, you must deploy an SSL certificate on your load balancer. The load balancer uses this certificate to terminate the connection and decrypt requests from clients before

24

sending them to the targets. For more information, see SSL Certificates. You must also specify the security policy that the load balancer uses to negotiate SSL connections with the clients. For more information, see Security Policies.

To configure a certificate and security policy

1. For **Select default certificate**, do one of the following:

   - If you created or imported a certificate using AWS Certificate Manager, select **Choose a certificate from ACM**, and then select the certificate from **Certificate name**.
   - If you uploaded a certificate using IAM, select **Choose a certificate from IAM**, and then select the certificate from **Certificate name**.

2. For **Security policy**, we recommend that you keep the default security policy.

3. Choose **Next: Configure Security Groups**.

Step 3: Configure a Security Group

The security group for your load balancer must allow it to communicate with registered targets on both the listener port and the health check port. The console can create a security group for your load balancer on your behalf with rules that allow this communication. If you prefer, you can create a security group and select it instead. For more information, see Recommended Rules.

To configure a security group for your load balancer

1. Choose **Create a new security group**.

2. Type a name and description for the security group, or keep the default name and description. This new security group contains a rule that allows traffic to the port that you selected for your load balancer on the **Configure Load Balancer** page.

3. Choose **Next: Configure Routing**.

Step 4: Configure a Target Group

You register targets with a target group. The target group that you configure in this step is used as the target group in the default listener rule, which forwards requests to the target group. For more information, see Target Groups for Your Application Load Balancers.

To configure your target group

1. For **Target group**, keep the default, **New target group**.

2. For **Name**, type a name for the target group.

3. Set **Protocol** and **Port** as needed.

4. For **Target type**, choose `instance` to specify targets by instance ID or `ip` to specify targets by IP address.

5. For **Health checks**, keep the default health check settings.

6. Choose **Next: Register Targets**.

Step 5: Configure Targets for the Target Group

With an Application Load Balancer, you will register targets by instance ID or by IP address, depending on the target type that you chose for your target group.

To register targets by instance ID

1. For **Instances**, select one or more instances.

2. Type the instance listener port, and then choose **Add to registered**.

3. When you have finished registering instances, choose **Next: Review**.

To register targets by IP address

1. For each IP address to register, do the following:

    1. For **Network**, if the IP address is from a subnet of the target group VPC, select the VPC. Otherwise, select **Other private IP address**.

    2. For **IP**, type the IP address.

    3. For **Port**, type the port.

    4. Choose **Add to list**.

2. When you have finished adding IP addresses to the list, choose **Next: Review**.

Step 6: Create the Load Balancer

After creating your load balancer, you can verify that your targets have passed the initial health check and then test that the load balancer is sending traffic to your targets. When you are finished with your load balancer, you can delete it. For more information, see Delete an Application Load Balancer.

To create the load balancer

1. On the **Review** page, choose **Create**.

2. After the load balancer is created, choose **Close**.

3. (Optional) To define additional listener rules that forward requests based on a path pattern or a hostname, see Add a Rule.

Availability Zones for Your Application Load Balancer

You can enable or disable the Availability Zones for your load balancer at any time. After you enable an Availability Zone, the load balancer starts routing requests to the registered targets in that Availability Zone. Your load balancer is most effective if you ensure that each enabled Availability Zone has at least one registered target.

After you disable an Availability Zone, the targets in that Availability Zone remain registered with the load balancer, but the load balancer will not route requests to them.

To update Availability Zones using the console

1. Open the Amazon EC2 console at https://console.aws.amazon.com/ec2/.
2. On the navigation pane, under **LOAD BALANCING**, choose **Load Balancers**.
3. Select the load balancer.
4. On the **Description** tab, under **Basic Configuration**, choose **Edit Availability Zones**.
5. To enable an Availability Zone, select the check box for that Availability Zone. If there is one subnet for that Availability Zone, it is selected. If there is more than one subnet for that Availability Zone, select one of the subnets. Note that you can select only one subnet per Availability Zone.
6. To change the subnet for an enabled Availability Zone, choose **Change subnet** and select one of the other subnets.
7. To remove an Availability Zone, clear the check box for that Availability Zone.
8. Choose **Save**.

To update Availability Zones using the AWS CLI
Use the set-subnets command.

Security Groups for Your Application Load Balancer

You must ensure that your load balancer can communicate with registered targets on both the listener port and the health check port. Whenever you add a listener to your load balancer or update the health check port for a target group used by the load balancer to route requests, you must verify that the security groups associated with the load balancer allow traffic on the new port in both directions. If they do not, you can edit the rules for the currently associated security groups or associate different security groups with the load balancer.

Recommended Rules

The recommended rules depend on the type of load balancer (Internet-facing or internal).

Internet-facing Load Balancer

Inbound
Source
0.0.0.0/0
Outbound
Destination
instance security group
instance security group

Internal Load Balancer

Inbound
Source
VPC CIDR
Outbound
Destination
instance security group
instance security group

We also recommend that you allow inbound ICMP traffic to support Path MTU Discovery. For more information, see Path MTU Discovery in the *Amazon EC2 User Guide for Linux Instances*.

Update the Associated Security Groups

You can update the security groups associated with your load balancer at any time.

To update security groups using the console

1. Open the Amazon EC2 console at https://console.aws.amazon.com/ec2/.

2. On the navigation pane, under **LOAD BALANCING**, choose **Load Balancers**.

3. Select the load balancer.

4. On the **Description** tab, under **Security**, choose **Edit security groups**.

5. To associate a security group with your load balancer, select it. To remove a security group from your load balancer, clear it.

6. Choose **Save**.

To update security groups using the AWS CLI

Use the set-security-groups command.

IP Address Types for Your Application Load Balancer

You can configure your Application Load Balancer to route IPv4 traffic only or to route both IPv4 and IPv6 traffic. For more information, see IP Address Type.

IPv6 Requirements

- An Internet-facing load balancer.
- Your virtual private cloud (VPC) has subnets with associated IPv6 CIDR blocks. For more information, see IPv6 Addresses in the *Amazon EC2 User Guide.*

To update the IP address type using the console

1. Open the Amazon EC2 console at https://console.aws.amazon.com/ec2/.

2. On the navigation pane, under **LOAD BALANCING**, choose **Load Balancers**.

3. Select the load balancer.

4. Choose **Actions, Edit IP address type**.

5. For **IP address type**, choose **ipv4** to support IPv4 addresses only or **dualstack** to support both IPv4 and IPv6 addresses.

6. Choose **Save**.

To update the IP address type using the AWS CLI
Use the set-ip-address-type command.

Tags for Your Application Load Balancer

Tags help you to categorize your load balancers in different ways, for example, by purpose, owner, or environment.

You can add multiple tags to each load balancer. Tag keys must be unique for each load balancer. If you add a tag with a key that is already associated with the load balancer, it updates the value of that tag.

When you are finished with a tag, you can remove it from your load balancer.

Restrictions

- Maximum number of tags per resource—50
- Maximum key length—127 Unicode characters
- Maximum value length—255 Unicode characters
- Tag keys and values are case sensitive. Allowed characters are letters, spaces, and numbers representable in UTF-8, plus the following special characters: + - = . _ : / @. Do not use leading or trailing spaces.
- Do not use the `aws:` prefix in your tag names or values because it is reserved for AWS use. You can't edit or delete tag names or values with this prefix. Tags with this prefix do not count against your tags per resource limit.

To update the tags for a load balancer using the console

1. Open the Amazon EC2 console at https://console.aws.amazon.com/ec2/.

2. On the navigation pane, under **LOAD BALANCING**, choose **Load Balancers**.

3. Select the load balancer.

4. On the **Tags** tab, choose **Add/Edit Tags**, and then do one or more of the following:

   1. To update a tag, edit the values of **Key** and **Value**.

   2. To add a new tag, choose **Create Tag** and then type values for **Key** and **Value**.

   3. To delete a tag, choose the delete icon (X) next to the tag.

5. When you have finished updating tags, choose **Save**.

To update the tags for a load balancer using the AWS CLI
Use the add-tags and remove-tags commands.

Delete an Application Load Balancer

As soon as your load balancer becomes available, you are billed for each hour or partial hour that you keep it running. When you no longer need the load balancer, you can delete it. As soon as the load balancer is deleted, you stop incurring charges for it.

You can't delete a load balancer if deletion protection is enabled. For more information, see Deletion Protection.

Note that deleting a load balancer does not affect its registered targets. For example, your EC2 instances continue to run and are still registered to their target groups. To delete your target groups, see Delete a Target Group.

To delete a load balancer using the console

1. If you have a CNAME record for your domain that points to your load balancer, point it to a new location and wait for the DNS change to take effect before deleting your load balancer.

2. Open the Amazon EC2 console at https://console.aws.amazon.com/ec2/.

3. On the navigation pane, under **LOAD BALANCING**, choose **Load Balancers**.

4. Select the load balancer, and then choose **Actions, Delete**.

5. When prompted for confirmation, choose **Yes, Delete**.

To delete a load balancer using the AWS CLI
Use the delete-load-balancer command.

Listeners for Your Application Load Balancers

Before you start using your Application Load Balancer, you must add one or more *listeners*. A listener is a process that checks for connection requests, using the protocol and port that you configure. The rules that you define for a listener determine how the load balancer routes requests to the targets in one or more target groups.

Topics

- Listener Configuration
- Listener Rules
- Host Conditions
- Path Conditions
- Create a Listener
- Configure HTTPS Listeners
- Update Listener Rules
- Update Server Certificates
- Authenticate Users
- Delete a Listener

Listener Configuration

Listeners support the following protocols and ports:

- **Protocols**: HTTP, HTTPS
- **Ports**: 1-65535

You can use an HTTPS listener to offload the work of encryption and decryption to your load balancer so that your applications can focus on their business logic. If the listener protocol is HTTPS, you must deploy exactly one SSL server certificate on the listener. For more information, see HTTPS Listeners for Your Application Load Balancer.

Application Load Balancers provide native support for Websockets. You can use WebSockets with both HTTP and HTTPS listeners.

Application Load Balancers provide native support for HTTP/2 with HTTPS listeners. You can send up to 128 requests in parallel using one HTTP/2 connection. The load balancer converts these to individual HTTP/1.1 requests and distributes them across the healthy targets in the target group using the round robin routing algorithm. Because HTTP/2 uses front-end connections more efficiently, you might notice fewer connections between clients and the load balancer. Note that you can't use the server-push feature of HTTP/2.

Listener Rules

Each listener has a default rule, and you can optionally define additional rules. Each rule consists of a priority, a forward action, an optional authenticate action (for HTTPS listeners), an optional host condition, and an optional path condition.

Default Rules

When you create a listener, you define actions for the default rule. Default rules can't have conditions. If no conditions for any of a listener's rules are met, then the action for the default rule is performed.

The following is an example of a default rule as shown in the console:

last	HTTP 80: default action	IF		THEN
	This rule cannot be moved or deleted	✔ Requests otherwise not routed		**Forward to** my-targets

Rule Priority

Each rule has a priority. Rules are evaluated in priority order, from the lowest value to the highest value. The default rule is evaluated last. You can change the priority of a nondefault rule at any time. You cannot change the priority of the default rule. For more information, see Reorder Rules.

Rule Actions

Each rule action has a type, an order, and information required to perform the action. The following are the supported action types:

`authenticate-cognito`
[HTTPS listeners] Use Amazon Cognito to authenticate users.

`authenticate-oidc`
[HTTPS listeners] Use an identity provider that is compliant with OpenID Connect (OIDC) to authenticate users.

`forward`
Forward requests to the specified target group.

The action with the lowest order value is performed first. Each rule must include one `forward` action. The `forward` action must be performed last. You can edit a rule at any time. For more information, see Edit a Rule.

Rule Conditions

There are two types of rule conditions: host and path. Each rule can have up to one host condition and up to one path condition. When the conditions for a rule are met, then its action is performed.

Host Conditions

You can use host conditions to define rules that forward requests to different target groups based on the host name in the host header (also known as *host-based routing*). This enables you to support multiple domains using a single load balancer.

Each host condition has one hostname. If the hostname in the host header matches the hostname in a listener rule exactly, the request is routed using that rule.

A hostname is case-insensitive, can be up to 128 characters in length, and can contain any of the following characters. Note that you can include up to three wildcard characters.

- A–Z, a–z, 0–9
- - .
- * (matches 0 or more characters)
- ? (matches exactly 1 character)

Example hostnames

- **example.com**
- **test.example.com**

- *.example.com

Note that ***.example.com** will match **test.example.com** but won't match **example.com**.

Console Example
The following is an example of a rule with a host condition as shown in the console. If the hostname in the host header matches ***.example.com**, the request is forwarded to the target group named **my-web-servers**. For more information, see Add a Rule.

1	ARN ⌄	IF		THEN
		✔ Host is *.example.com		**Forward to** my-web-servers

Path Conditions

You can use path conditions to define rules that forward requests to different target groups based on the URL in the request (also known as *path-based routing*).

Each path condition has one path pattern. If the URL in a request matches the path pattern in a listener rule exactly, the request is routed using that rule.

A path pattern is case-sensitive, can be up to 128 characters in length, and can contain any of the following characters. Note that you can include up to three wildcard characters.

- A–Z, a–z, 0–9
- _ - . $ / ~ " ' @ : +
- & (using &)
- * (matches 0 or more characters)
- ? (matches exactly 1 character)

Example path patterns
- /img/*
- /js/*

Note that the path pattern is used to route requests but does not alter them. For example, if a rule has a path pattern of /img/*, the rule would forward a request for /img/picture.jpg to the specified target group as a request for /img/picture.jpg.

Console Example
The following is an example of a rule with a path condition as shown in the console. If the URL in the request matches /img/*, the request is forwarded to the target group named **my-targets**. For more information, see Add a Rule.

2	ARN ⌄	IF		THEN
		✔ Path is /img/*		**Forward to** my-targets

Create a Listener for Your Application Load Balancer

A listener is a process that checks for connection requests. You define a listener when you create your load balancer, and you can add listeners to your load balancer at any time.

Prerequisites

- You must specify a target group for the default listener rule. For more information, see Create a Target Group.
- If you create an HTTPS listener, you must specify a certificate and a security policy. The load balancer uses the certificate to terminate the connection and decrypt requests from clients before routing them to targets. For more information, see SSL Certificates. The load balancer uses the security policy when negotiating SSL connections with the clients. For more information, see Security Policies.

Add a Listener

You configure a listener with a protocol and a port for connections from clients to the load balancer, and a target group for the default listener rule. For more information, see Listener Configuration.

To add a listener using the console

1. Open the Amazon EC2 console at https://console.aws.amazon.com/ec2/.

2. On the navigation pane, under **LOAD BALANCING**, choose **Load Balancers**.

3. Select a load balancer, and choose **Listeners**, **Add listener**.

4. For **Protocol : port**, choose **HTTP** or **HTTPS**. Keep the default port or type a different port.

5. (Optional, HTTPS listeners) To authenticate users, for **Default actions**, choose **Add action**, **Authenticate** and provide the requested information. To save the action, choose the checkmark icon. For more information, see Authenticate Users Using an Application Load Balancer.

6. For **Default actions**, choose **Add action**, **Forward to** and choose a target group. To save the action, choose the checkmark icon.

7. [HTTPS listeners] For **Security policy**, we recommend that you keep the default security policy.

8. [HTTPS listeners] For **Default SSL certificate**, do one of the following:

   - If you created or imported a certificate using AWS Certificate Manager, choose **From ACM** and choose the certificate.
   - If you uploaded a certificate using IAM, choose **From IAM** and choose the certificate.

9. Choose **Save**.

10. (Optional) To define additional listener rules that forward requests based on a path pattern or a hostname, see Add a Rule.

To add a listener using the AWS CLI

Use the create-listener command to create the listener and default rule, and the create-rule command to define additional listener rules.

HTTPS Listeners for Your Application Load Balancer

You can create a listener that uses encrypted connections (also known as *SSL offload*). This feature enables traffic encryption between your load balancer and the clients that initiate SSL or TLS sessions.

To use an HTTPS listener, you must deploy an SSL/TLS server certificate on your load balancer. The load balancer uses this certificate to terminate the connection and then decrypt requests from clients before sending them to the targets.

Elastic Load Balancing uses a Secure Socket Layer (SSL) negotiation configuration, known as a security policy, to negotiate SSL connections between a client and the load balancer. A security policy is a combination of protocols and ciphers. The protocol establishes a secure connection between a client and a server and ensures that all data passed between the client and your load balancer is private. A cipher is an encryption algorithm that uses encryption keys to create a coded message. Protocols use several ciphers to encrypt data over the Internet. During the connection negotiation process, the client and the load balancer present a list of ciphers and protocols that they each support, in order of preference. By default, the first cipher on the server's list that matches any one of the client's ciphers is selected for the secure connection.

SSL Certificates

The load balancer uses an X.509 certificate (SSL/TLS server certificate). Certificates are a digital form of identification issued by a certificate authority (CA). A certificate contains identification information, a validity period, a public key, a serial number, and the digital signature of the issuer.

When you create a certificate for use with your load balancer, you must specify a domain name.

We recommend that you create certificates for your load balancer using AWS Certificate Manager (ACM). ACM integrates with Elastic Load Balancing so that you can deploy the certificate on your load balancer. For more information, see the AWS Certificate Manager User Guide.

Alternatively, you can use SSL/TLS tools to create a certificate signing request (CSR), then get the CSR signed by a CA to produce a certificate, then import the certificate into ACM or upload the certificate to AWS Identity and Access Management (IAM). For more information about importing certificates into ACM, see Importing Certificates in the *AWS Certificate Manager User Guide*. For more information about uploading certificates to IAM, see Working with Server Certificates in the *IAM User Guide*.

Important
You cannot install certificates with 4096-bit RSA keys or EC keys on your load balancer through integration with ACM. You must upload certificates with 4096-bit RSA keys or EC keys to IAM in order to use them with your load balancer.

When you create an HTTPS listener, you specify a default certificate. You can create an optional certificate list for the listener by adding more certificates. This enables a load balancer to support multiple domains on the same port and provide a different certificate for each domain. For more information, see Update Server Certificates.

Clients can use the Server Name Identification (SNI) protocol extension to specify the hostname they are trying to reach. If the hostname doesn't match a certificate, the load balancer selects the default certificate. If the hostname matches a single certificate, the load balancer selects this certificate. If a hostname provided by a client matches multiple certificates, the load balancer selects the best certificate that the client can support. Certificate selection is based on the following criteria in the following order:

- Public key algorithm (prefer ECDSA over RSA)
- Hashing algorithm (prefer SHA over MD5)
- Key length (prefer the largest)
- Validity period

The load balancer access log entries indicate the hostname specified by the client and the certificate presented to the client. For more information, see Access Log Entries.

Security Policies

You can choose the security policy that is used for front-end connections. The `ELBSecurityPolicy-2016-08` security policy is always used for backend connections. Application Load Balancers do not support custom security policies.

Elastic Load Balancing provides the following security policies for Application Load Balancers:

- `ELBSecurityPolicy-2016-08`
- `ELBSecurityPolicy-TLS-1-2-2017-01`
- `ELBSecurityPolicy-TLS-1-1-2017-01`
- `ELBSecurityPolicy-2015-05`
- `ELBSecurityPolicy-TLS-1-0-2015-04`

We recommend the `ELBSecurityPolicy-2016-08` policy for general use. You can use one of the `ELBSecurityPolicy-TLS` policies to meet compliance and security standards that require disabling certain TLS protocol versions, or to support legacy clients that require deprecated ciphers. Note that only a small percentage of Internet clients require TLS version 1.0. To view the TLS protocol version for requests to your load balancer, enable access logging for your load balancer and examine the access logs. For more information, see Access Logs.

The following table describes the security policies defined for Application Load Balancers.

Security Policy	2016-08 *	TLS-1-1-2017-01	TLS-1-2-2017-01	TLS-1-0-2015-04 †
TLS Protocols				
Protocol-TLSv1				
Protocol-TLSv1.1				
Protocol-TLSv1.2				
TLS Ciphers				
ECDHE-ECDSA-AES128-GCM-SHA256				
ECDHE-RSA-AES128-GCM-SHA256				
ECDHE-ECDSA-AES128-SHA256				
ECDHE-RSA-AES128-SHA256				
ECDHE-ECDSA-AES128-SHA				
ECDHE-RSA-AES128-SHA				
ECDHE-ECDSA-AES256-GCM-SHA384				
ECDHE-RSA-AES256-GCM-SHA384				
ECDHE-ECDSA-AES256-SHA384				

Security Policy	2016-08 *	TLS-1-1-2017-01	TLS-1-2-2017-01	TLS-1-0-2015-04 †
ECDHE-RSA-AES256-SHA384				
ECDHE-RSA-AES256-SHA				
ECDHE-ECDSA-AES256-SHA				
AES128-GCM-SHA256				
AES128-SHA256				
AES128-SHA				
AES256-GCM-SHA384				
AES256-SHA256				
AES256-SHA				
DES-CBC3-SHA				

* The `ELBSecurityPolicy-2016-08` and `ELBSecurityPolicy-2015-05` security policies for Application Load Balancers are identical.

† Do not use this security policy unless you must support a legacy client that requires the DES-CBC3-SHA cipher, which is a weak cipher.

To view the configuration of a security policy for Application Load Balancers using the AWS CLI, use the describe-ssl-policies command.

Update the Security Policy

When you create an HTTPS listener, you can select the security policy that meets your needs. When a new security policy is added, you can update your HTTPS listener to use the new security policy. Note that Application Load Balancers do not support custom security policies.

To update the security policy using the console

1. Open the Amazon EC2 console at https://console.aws.amazon.com/ec2/.

2. On the navigation pane, under **LOAD BALANCING**, choose **Load Balancers**.

3. Select the load balancer and choose **Listeners**.

4. Select the checkbox for the HTTPS listener and choose **Edit**.

5. For **Security policy**, choose a security policy.

6. Choose **Update**.

To update the security policy using the AWS CLI
Use the modify-listener command.

Listener Rules for Your Application Load Balancer

The rules that you define for your listener determine how the load balancer routes requests to the targets in one or more target groups.

Each rule consists of a priority, one or more actions, an optional host condition, and an optional path condition. For more information, see Listener Rules.

Note
The console displays a relative sequence number for each rule, not the rule priority. You can get the priority of a rule by describing it using the AWS CLI or the Elastic Load Balancing API.

Prerequisites

A rule routes requests to its target group. Before you create a rule or update the target group for a rule, create the target group and add targets to it. For more information, see Create a Target Group.

Add a Rule

You define a default rule when you create a listener, and you can define additional nondefault rules at any time.

To add a rule using the console

1. Open the Amazon EC2 console at https://console.aws.amazon.com/ec2/.

2. On the navigation pane, under **LOAD BALANCING**, choose **Load Balancers**.

3. Select the load balancer and choose **Listeners**.

4. For the listener to update, choose **View/edit rules**.

5. Choose the **Add rules** icon (the plus sign) in the menu bar, which adds **Insert Rule** icons at the locations where you can insert a rule in the priority order.

Click a location for your new rule. Each rule must include a forward action.

6. Define the rule as follows:

   1. Choose **Insert Rule**.

   2. (Optional) To configure host-based routing, choose **Add condition**, **Host is** and type the hostname (for example, ***.example.com**). To save the condition, choose the checkmark icon

   3. (Optional) To configure path-based routing, choose **Add condition**, **Path is** and type the path pattern (for example, **/img/***). To save the condition, choose the checkmark icon.

   4. (Optional, HTTPS listeners) To authenticate users, choose **Add action**, **Authenticate** and provide the requested information. For more information, see Authenticate Users Using an Application Load Balancer.

   5. To add a forward action, choose **Add action**, **Forward to** and choose a target group. Each rule must have exactly one forward action.

   6. (Optional) To change the order of the rule, use the arrows. The default rule always has the **last** priority.

7. Choose **Save**.

7. To leave this screen, choose the **Back to the load balancer** icon (the back button) in the menu bar.

To add a rule using the AWS CLI

Use the create-rule command to create the rule. Use the describe-rules command to view information about the rule.

Edit a Rule

You can edit the action and conditions for a rule at any time.

To edit a rule using the console

1. Open the Amazon EC2 console at https://console.aws.amazon.com/ec2/.

2. On the navigation pane, under **LOAD BALANCING**, choose **Load Balancers**.

3. Select the load balancer and choose **Listeners**.

4. For the listener to update, choose **View/edit rules**.

5. Choose the **Edit rules** icon (the pencil) in the menu bar.

Select the rule to edit. Each rule must include a forward action.

6. For the rule to edit, choose the **Edit rules** icon (the pencil).

7. (Optional) Modify the conditions and actions as needed. For example, you can edit a condition or action (pencil icon), add a path condition if you don't have one already, add a host condition if you don't have one already, add an authenticate action for a rule for an HTTPS listener, or delete a condition or action (trash can icon). You can't add conditions to the default rule. Each rule must have exactly one forward action.

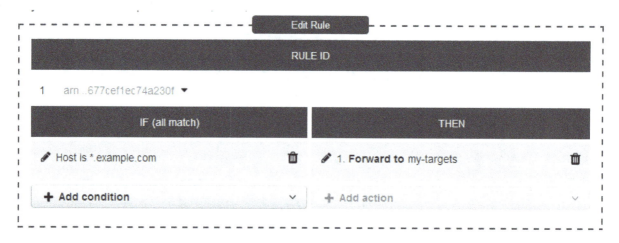

8. Choose **Update**.

9. To leave this screen, choose the **Back to the load balancer** icon (the back button) in the menu bar.

To edit a rule using the AWS CLI
Use the modify-rule command.

Reorder Rules

Rules are evaluated in priority order, from the lowest value to the highest value. The default rule is evaluated last. You can change the priority of a nondefault rule at any time. You cannot change the priority of the default rule.

Note
The console displays a relative sequence number for each rule, not the rule priority. When you reorder rules using the console, they get new rule priorities based on the existing rule priorities. To set the priority of a rule to a specific value, use the AWS CLI or the Elastic Load Balancing API.

To reorder rules using the console

1. Open the Amazon EC2 console at https://console.aws.amazon.com/ec2/.

2. On the navigation pane, under **LOAD BALANCING**, choose **Load Balancers**.

3. Select the load balancer and choose **Listeners**.

4. For the listener to update, choose **View/edit rules**.

5. Choose the **Reorder rules** icon (the arrows) in the menu bar.

6. Select the check box next to a rule, and then use the arrows to give the rule a new priority. Note that the default rule always has the last priority.

7. When you have finished reordering rules, choose **Save**.

8. To leave this screen, choose the **Back to the load balancer** icon (the back button) in the menu bar.

To update rule priorities using the AWS CLI
Use the set-rule-priorities command.

Delete a Rule

You can delete the nondefault rules for a listener at any time. You cannot delete the default rule for a listener. When you delete a listener, all its rules are deleted.

To delete a rule using the console

1. Open the Amazon EC2 console at https://console.aws.amazon.com/ec2/.

2. On the navigation pane, under **LOAD BALANCING**, choose **Load Balancers**.

3. Select the load balancer and choose **Listeners**.

4. For the listener to update, choose **View/edit rules**.

5. Choose the **Delete rules** icon (the minus sign) in the menu bar.

6. Select the check box for the rule and choose **Delete**. Note that you can't delete the default rule for the listener.

7. To leave this screen, choose the **Back to the load balancer** icon (the back button) in the menu bar.

To delete a rule using the AWS CLI

Use the delete-rule command.

Update Server Certificates

When you create an HTTPS listener, you specify a default certificate. You can also create a certificate list for the listener by adding additional certificates.

Each certificate comes with a validity period. You must ensure that you renew or replace the certificate before its validity period ends. Renewing or replacing a certificate does not affect in-flight requests that were received by the load balancer node and are pending routing to a healthy target. After a certificate is renewed, new requests use the renewed certificate. After a certificate is replaced, new requests use the new certificate.

You can manage certificate renewal and replacement as follows:

- Certificates provided by AWS Certificate Manager and deployed on your load balancer can be renewed automatically. ACM attempts to renew certificates before they expire. For more information, see Managed Renewal in the *AWS Certificate Manager User Guide*.
- If you imported a certificate into ACM, you must monitor the expiration date of the certificate and renew it before it expires. For more information, see Importing Certificates in the *AWS Certificate Manager User Guide*.
- If you imported a certificate into IAM, you must create a new certificate, import the new certificate to ACM or IAM, add the new certificate to your load balancer, and remove the expired certificate from your load balancer.

Limitation
ACM supports RSA certificates with a 4096 key length and EC certificates. However, you cannot install these certificates on your load balancer through integration with ACM. You must upload these certificates to IAM in order to use them with your load balancer.

Add Certificates

You can add certificates to the certificate list for your listener using the following procedure. The default certificate for a listener is not added to the certificate list by default, but you can add the default certificate to the certificate list.

To add certificates using the console

1. Open the Amazon EC2 console at https://console.aws.amazon.com/ec2/.

2. On the navigation pane, under **LOAD BALANCING**, choose **Load Balancers**.

3. Select the load balancer and choose **Listeners**.

4. For the HTTPS listener to update, choose **View/edit certificates**, which displays the default certificate followed by any other certificates that you've added to the listener.

5. Choose the **Add certificates** icon (the plus sign) in the menu bar, which displays the default certificate followed by any other certificates managed by ACM and IAM. If you've already added a certificate to the listener, its checkbox is selected and disabled.

6. To add certificates that are already managed by ACM or IAM, select the checkboxes for the certificates and choose **Add**.

7. If you have a certificate that isn't managed by ACM or IAM, import it to ACM and add it to your listener as follows:

   1. Choose **Import certificate**.

   2. For **Certificate private key**, paste the PEM-encoded, unencrypted private key for the certificate.

   3. For **Certificate body**, paste the PEM-encoded certificate.

   4. (Optional) For **Certificate chain**, paste the PEM-encoded certificate chain.

5. Choose **Import**. The newly imported certificate appears in the list of available certificates and is selected.

6. Choose **Add**.

8. To leave this screen, choose the **Back to the load balancer** icon (the back button) in the menu bar.

To add a certificate using the AWS CLI
Use the add-listener-certificates command.

Replace the Default Certificate

You can replace the default certificate for your listener using the following procedure.

To change the default certificate using the console

1. Open the Amazon EC2 console at https://console.aws.amazon.com/ec2/.

2. On the navigation pane, under **LOAD BALANCING**, choose **Load Balancers**.

3. Select the load balancer and choose **Listeners**.

4. Select the checkbox for the listener and choose **Edit**.

5. For **Default SSL certificate**, do one of the following:

    - If you created or imported a certificate using AWS Certificate Manager, choose **From ACM** and choose the certificate.
    - If you uploaded a certificate using IAM, choose **From IAM** and choose the certificate.

6. Choose **Save**.

To change the default certificate using the AWS CLI
Use the modify-listener command.

Remove Certificates

You can remove the nondefault certificates for an HTTPS listener at any time. You cannot remove the default certificate for an HTTPS listener using this procedure.

To remove certificates using the console

1. Open the Amazon EC2 console at https://console.aws.amazon.com/ec2/.

2. On the navigation pane, under **LOAD BALANCING**, choose **Load Balancers**.

3. Select the load balancer and choose **Listeners**.

4. For the listener to update, choose **View/edit certificates**, which displays the default certificate followed by any other certificates that you've added to the listener.

5. Choose the **Remove certificates** icon (the minus sign) in the menu bar.

6. Select the checkboxes for the certificates and choose **Remove**.

7. To leave this screen, choose the **Back to the load balancer** icon (the back button) in the menu bar.

To remove a certificate using the AWS CLI
Use the remove-listener-certificates command.

Authenticate Users Using an Application Load Balancer

You can configure an Application Load Balancer to securely authenticate users as they access your applications. This enables you to offload the work of authenticating users to your load balancer so that your applications can focus on their business logic.

The following use cases are supported:

- Authenticate users through an identity provider (IdP) that is OpenID Connect (OIDC) compliant.
- Authenticate users through well-known social IdPs, such as Amazon, Facebook, or Google, through the user pools supported by Amazon Cognito.
- Authenticate users through corporate identities, using SAML, LDAP, or Microsoft AD, through the user pools supported by Amazon Cognito.

Prepare to Use an OIDC-Compliant IdP

Do the following if you are using an OIDC-compliant IdP with your Application Load Balancer:

- Create a new OIDC app in your IdP. You must configure a client ID and a client secret.
- Get the following endpoints published by the IdP: authorization endpoint, token endpoint, and user info endpoint. You can locate this information in the well-known config.
- Whitelist one of the following redirect URLs in your IdP app, whichever your users will use, where DNS is the domain name of your load balancer and CNAME is the DNS alias for your application.
    - https://*DNS*/oauth2/idpresponse
    - https://*CNAME*/oauth2/idpresponse

Prepare to Use Amazon Cognito

Do the following if you are using Amazon Cognito user pools with your Application Load Balancer:

- Create a user pool. For more information, see Amazon Cognito User Pools in the *Amazon Cognito Developer Guide.*
- Create a user pool client. You must configure the client to generate a client secret, use code grant flow, and support the same OAuth scopes that the load balancer uses. For more information, see Configuring a User Pool App Client in the *Amazon Cognito Developer Guide.*
- Create a user pool domain. For more information, see Adding a Domain Name for Your User Pool in the *Amazon Cognito Developer Guide.*
- To federate with a social or corporate IdP, enable the IdP in the federation section. For more information, see Add Social Sign-in to a User Pool or Add Sign-in with a SAML IdP to a User Pool in the *Amazon Cognito Developer Guide.*
- Whitelist the following redirect URLs in the callback URL field for Amazon Cognito, where DNS is the domain name of your load balancer, and CNAME is the DNS alias for your application (if you are using one).
    - https://*DNS*/oauth2/idpresponse
    - https://*CNAME*/oauth2/idpresponse
- Whitelist your user pool domain on your IdP app's callback URL. Use the format for your IdP. For example:
    - https://*domain-prefix*.auth.*region*.amazoncognito.com/saml2/idpresponse
    - https://*user-pool-domain*/oauth2/idpresponse

To enable an IAM user to configure a load balancer to use Amazon Cognito to authenticate users, you must grant the user permission to call the `cognito-idp:DescribeUserPoolClient` action.

Configure User Authentication

You configure user authentication by creating an authenticate action for one or more listener rules. The `authenticate-cognito` and `authenticate-oidc` action types are supported only with HTTPS listeners. For descriptions of the corresponding fields, see AuthenticateCognitoActionConfig and AuthenticateOidcActionConfig in the *Elastic Load Balancing API Reference version 2015-12-01*.

By default, the `SessionTimeout` field is set to 7 days. If you want shorter sessions, you can configure a session timeout as short as 1 second. For more information, see Authentication Logout and Session Timeout.

Set the `OnUnauthenticatedRequest` field as appropriate for your application. For example:

- **Applications that require the user to log in using a social or corporate identity**—This is supported by the default option, `authenticate`. If the user is not logged in, the load balancer redirects the request to the IdP authorization endpoint and the IdP prompts the user to log in using its user interface.
- **Applications that provide a personalized view to a user that is logged in or a general view to a user that is not logged in**—To support this type of application, use the `allow` option. If the user is logged in, the load balancer provides the user claims and the application can provide a personalized view. If the user is not logged in, the load balancer forwards the request without the user claims and the application can provide the general view.
- **Single-page applications with JavaScript that loads every few seconds**—By default, after the authentication session cookie expires, the AJAX calls are redirected to the IdP and are blocked. If you use the `deny` option, the load balancer returns an HTTP 401 Unauthorized error to these AJAX calls.

The load balancer must be able to communicate with the IdP token endpoint (`TokenEndpoint`) and the IdP user info endpoint (`UserInfoEndpoint`). Verify that the security groups for your load balancer and the network ACLs for your VPC allow outbound access to these endpoints.

Use the following create-rule command to configure user authentication.

```
1 aws elbv2 create-rule --listener-arn listener-arn --priority 10 \
2 --conditions Field=path-pattern,Values="/login" --actions file://actions.json
```

The following is an example of the `actions.json` file that specifies an `authenticate-oidc` action and a `forward` action.

```
1 [{
2     "Type": "authenticate-oidc",
3     "AuthenticateOidcConfig": {
4         "Issuer": "https://idp-issuer.com",
5         "AuthorizationEndpoint": "https://authorization-endpoint.com",
6         "TokenEndpoint": "https://token-endpoint.com",
7         "UserInfoEndpoint": "https://user-info-endpoint.com",
8         "ClientId": "abcdefghijklmnopqrstuvwxyz123456789",
9         "ClientSecret": "123456789012345678901234567890",
10        "SessionCookieName": "my-cookie",
11        "SessionTimeout": 3600,
12        "Scope": "email",
13        "AuthenticationRequestExtraParams": {
14            "display": "page",
15            "prompt": "login"
16        },
17        "OnUnauthenticatedRequest": "deny"
18    },
19    "Order": 1
20 },
21 {
22     "Type": "forward",
```

```
23    "TargetGroupArn": "arn:aws:elasticloadbalancing:region-code:account-id:targetgroup/target-
          group-name/target-group-id",
24    "Order": 2
25  }]
```

The following is an example of the `actions.json` file that specifies an `authenticate-cognito` action and a `forward` action.

```
1  [{
2    "Type": "authenticate-cognito",
3    "AuthenticateCognitoConfig": {
4      "UserPoolArn": "arn:aws:cognito-idp:region-code:account-id:userpool/user-pool-id",
5      "UserPoolClientId": "abcdefghijklmnopqrstuvwxyz123456789",
6      "UserPoolDomain": "userPoolDomain1",
7      "SessionCookieName": "my-cookie",
8      "SessionTimeout": 3600,
9      "Scope": "email",
10      "AuthenticationRequestExtraParams": {
11        "display": "page",
12        "prompt": "login"
13      },
14      "OnUnauthenticatedRequest": "deny"
15    },
16    "Order": 1
17  },
18  {
19    "Type": "forward",
20    "TargetGroupArn": "arn:aws:elasticloadbalancing:region-code:account-id:targetgroup/target-
          group-name/target-group-id",
21    "Order": 2
22  }]
```

For more information, see Listener Rules.

Authentication Flow

Elastic Load Balancing uses the OIDC authorization code flow, which includes the following steps.

1. When the conditions for a rule with an authenticate action are met, the load balancer checks for an authentication session cookie in the request headers. If the cookie is not present, the load balancer redirects the user to the IdP authorization endpoint so that the IdP can authenticate the user.

2. After the user is authenticated, the IdP redirects the user back to the load balancer with a authorization grant code. The load balancer presents the code to the IdP token endpoint to get the ID token and access token.

3. After the load balancer validates the ID token, it exchanges the access token with the IdP user info endpoint to get the user claims.

4. The load balancer creates the authentication session cookie and sends it to the client so that the client's user agent can send the cookie to the load balancer when making requests. Because most browsers limit a cookie to 4K in size, the load balancer shards a cookie that is greater than 4K in size into multiple cookies. If the total size of the user claims and access token received from the IdP is greater than 11K in size, the load balancer returns an error.

5. The load balancer sends the user claims to the target in HTTP headers. For more information, see User Claims Encoding and Signature Verification.

48

6. If the IdP provides a valid refresh token in the ID token, the load balancer saves the refresh token and uses it to refresh the user claims each time the access token expires, until the session times out or the IdP refresh fails. If the user logs out, the refresh fails and the load balancer redirects the user to the IdP authorization endpoint. This enables the load balancer to drop sessions after the user logs out. For more information, see Authentication Logout and Session Timeout.

User Claims Encoding and Signature Verification

After your load balancer authenticates a user successfully, it sends the user claims received from the IdP to the target. The load balancer signs the user claim so that applications can verify the signature and verify that the claims were sent by the load balancer.

The load balancer adds the following HTTP headers:

x-amzn-oidc-accesstoken
The access token from the token endpoint, in clear text.

x-amzn-oidc-identity
The subject field (sub) from the user info endpoint, in clear text.

x-amzn-oidc-data
The user claims, in JSON web tokens (JWT) format.

Applications that require the full user claims can use any standard JWT library. The JWT format includes a header, payload, and signature that are Base64 URL encoded. The JWT signature is ECDSA + P-256 + SHA256.

The JWT header is a JSON object with the following fields.

```
1 {
2     "alg": "algorithm",
3     "kid": "12345678-1234-1234-1234-123456789012",
4     "signer": "arn:aws:elasticloadbalancing:region-code:account-id:loadbalancer/app/load-balancer
            -name/load-balancer-id",
5     "iss": "url",
6     "client": "client-id",
7     "exp": "expiration"
8 }
```

The JWT payload is a JSON object that contains the user claims received from the IdP user info endpoint.

```
1 {
2     "sub": "1234567890",
3     "name": "name",
4     "email": "alias@example.com",
5     ...
6 }
```

Because the load balancer does not encrypt the user claims, we recommend that you configure the target group to use HTTPS. If you configure your target group to use HTTP, be sure to restrict the traffic to your load balancer using security groups. We also recommend that you verify the signature before doing any authorization based on the claims. To get the public key, get the key ID from the JWT header and use it to look up the public key from the following regional endpoint:

```
1 https://public-keys.auth.elb.region.amazonaws.com/key-id
```

For AWS GovCloud (US), the endpoint is as follows:

```
1 https://s3-us-gov-west-1.amazonaws.com/aws-elb-public-keys-prod-us-gov-west-1/key-id
```

The following example shows how to get the public key in Python.

```python
1  import jwt
2  import requests
3
4  # Step 1: Get the key id from JWT headers (the kid field)
5  encoded_jwt = headers.dict['x-amzn-oidc-data']
6  jwt_headers = encoded_jwt.split('.')[0]
7  decoded_jwt_headers = base64.b64decode(jwt_headers)
8  decoded_json = json.loads(decoded_jwt_headers)
9  kid = decoded_json['kid']
10
11 # Step 2: Get the public key from regional endpoint
12 url = 'https://public-keys.auth.elb' + region + '.amazonaws.com/' + kid
13 req = requests.get(url)
14 pub_key = req.text
15
16 # Step 3: Get the payload
17 payload = jwt.decode(encoded_jwt, pub_key, algorithms=['ES256'])
```

Authentication Logout and Session Timeout

When an application needs to log out an authenticated user, it should set the expiration time of the authentication session cookie to -1 and redirect the client to the IdP logout endpoint (if the IdP supports one). To prevent users from reusing a deleted cookie, we recommend that you configure as short an expiration time for the access token as is reasonable. If a client provides a load balancer with an authorization session cookie that has an expired access token with a non-NULL refresh token, the load balancer contacts the IdP to determine whether the user is still logged in.

The refresh token and the session timeout work together as follows:

- If the session timeout is shorter than the access token expiration, the load balancer honors the session timeout and has the user log in again after the authentication session times out.
- If the session timeout is longer than the access token expiration and the IdP does not support refresh tokens, the load balancer keeps the authentication session until it times out and then has the user log in again.
- If the session timeout is longer than the access token expiration and the IdP supports refresh tokens, the load balancer refreshes the user session each time the access token expires. The load balancer has the user log in again only after the authentication session times out or the refresh flow fails.

Delete a Listener for Your Application Load Balancer

You can delete a listener at any time. When you delete a load balancer, all its listeners are deleted.

To delete a listener using the console

1. Open the Amazon EC2 console at https://console.aws.amazon.com/ec2/.

2. On the navigation pane, under **LOAD BALANCING**, choose **Load Balancers**.

3. Select the load balancer and choose **Listeners**.

4. Select the checkbox for the HTTPS listener and choose **Delete**.

5. When prompted for confirmation, choose **Yes, Delete**.

To delete a listener using the AWS CLI
Use the delete-listener command.

Target Groups for Your Application Load Balancers

Each *target group* is used to route requests to one or more registered targets. When you create each listener rule, you specify a target group and conditions. When a rule condition is met, traffic is forwarded to the corresponding target group. You can create different target groups for different types of requests. For example, create one target group for general requests and other target groups for requests to the microservices for your application. For more information, see Application Load Balancer Components.

You define health check settings for your load balancer on a per target group basis. Each target group uses the default health check settings, unless you override them when you create the target group or modify them later on. After you specify a target group in a rule for a listener, the load balancer continually monitors the health of all targets registered with the target group that are in an Availability Zone enabled for the load balancer. The load balancer routes requests to the registered targets that are healthy.

Topics

- Routing Configuration
- Target Type
- Registered Targets
- Target Group Attributes
- Deregistration Delay
- Slow Start Mode
- Sticky Sessions
- Create a Target Group
- Health Checks for Your Target Groups
- Register Targets with Your Target Group
- Tags for Your Target Group
- Delete a Target Group

Routing Configuration

By default, a load balancer routes requests to its targets using the protocol and port number that you specified when you created the target group. Alternatively, you can override the port used for routing traffic to a target when you register it with the target group.

Target groups support the following protocols and ports:

- **Protocols**: HTTP, HTTPS
- **Ports**: 1-65535

If a target group is configured with the HTTPS protocol or uses HTTPS health checks, SSL connections to the targets use the security settings from the `ELBSecurityPolicy2016-08` policy.

Target Type

When you create a target group, you specify its target type, which determines how you specify its targets. After you create a target group, you cannot change its target type.

The following are the possible target types:

`instance`
The targets are specified by instance ID.

`ip`
The targets are specified by IP address.

When the target type is `ip`, you can specify IP addresses from one of the following CIDR blocks:

- The subnets of the VPC for the target group
- 10.0.0.0/8 (RFC 1918)
- 100.64.0.0/10 (RFC 6598)
- 172.16.0.0/12 (RFC 1918)
- 192.168.0.0/16 (RFC 1918)

These supported CIDR blocks enable you to register the following with a target group: ClassicLink instances, instances in a peered VPC, AWS resources that are addressable by IP address and port (for example, databases), and on-premises resources linked to AWS through AWS Direct Connect or a VPN connection.

Important
You can't specify publicly routable IP addresses.

If you specify targets using an instance ID, traffic is routed to instances using the primary private IP address specified in the primary network interface for the instance. If you specify targets using IP addresses, you can route traffic to an instance using any private IP address from one or more network interfaces. This enables multiple applications on an instance to use the same port. Each network interface can have its own security group.

Registered Targets

Your load balancer serves as a single point of contact for clients and distributes incoming traffic across its healthy registered targets. You can register each target with one or more target groups. You can register each EC2 instance or IP address with the same target group multiple times using different ports, which enables the load balancer to route requests to microservices.

If demand on your application increases, you can register additional targets with one or more target groups in order to handle the demand. The load balancer starts routing requests to a newly registered target as soon as the registration process completes and the target passes the initial health checks.

If demand on your application decreases, or you need to service your targets, you can deregister targets from your target groups. Deregistering a target removes it from your target group, but does not affect the target otherwise. The load balancer stops routing requests to a target as soon as it is deregistered. The target enters the `draining` state until in-flight requests have completed. You can register the target with the target group again when you are ready for it to resume receiving requests.

If you are registering targets by instance ID, you can use your load balancer with an Auto Scaling group. After you attach a target group to an Auto Scaling group, Auto Scaling registers your targets with the target group for you when it launches them. For more information, see Attaching a Load Balancer to Your Auto Scaling Group in the *Amazon EC2 Auto Scaling User Guide*.

Target Group Attributes

The following are the target group attributes:

`deregistration_delay.timeout_seconds`
The amount of time for Elastic Load Balancing to wait before deregistering a target. The range is 0–3600 seconds. The default value is 300 seconds.

`slow_start.duration_seconds`
The time period, in seconds, during which the load balancer sends a newly registered target a linearly increasing share of the traffic to the target group. The range is 30–900 seconds (15 minutes). The default is 0 seconds (disabled).

`stickiness.enabled`
Indicates whether sticky sessions are enabled.

`stickiness.lb_cookie.duration_seconds`
The cookie expiration period, in seconds. After this period, the cookie is considered stale. The minimum value is 1 second and the maximum value is 7 days (604800 seconds). The default value is 1 day (86400 seconds).

`stickiness.type`
The type of stickiness. The possible value is `lb_cookie`.

Deregistration Delay

Elastic Load Balancing stops sending requests to targets that are deregistering. By default, Elastic Load Balancing waits 300 seconds before completing the deregistration process, which can help in-flight requests to the target to complete. To change the amount of time that Elastic Load Balancing waits, update the deregistration delay value. You can specify a value of up to 1 hour, and that Elastic Load Balancing waits the full amount of time specified, regardless of whether there are in-flight requests.

If a deregistering target terminates the connection before the deregistration delay elapses, the client receives a 500-level error response.

The initial state of a deregistering target is `draining`. After the deregistration delay elapses, the deregistration process completes and the state of the target is `unused`. If the target is part of an Auto Scaling group, it can be terminated and replaced.

To update the deregistration delay value using the console

1. Open the Amazon EC2 console at https://console.aws.amazon.com/ec2/.

2. On the navigation pane, under **LOAD BALANCING**, choose **Target Groups**.

3. Select the target group. The current value is displayed on the **Description** tab as **Deregistration delay**.

4. On the **Description** tab, choose **Edit attributes**.

5. On the **Edit attributes** page, change the value of **Deregistration delay** as needed, and then choose **Save**.

To update the deregistration delay value using the AWS CLI
Use the modify-target-group-attributes command with the `deregistration_delay.timeout_seconds` attribute.

Slow Start Mode

By default, a target starts to receive its full share of requests as soon as it is registered with a target group and passes an initial health check. Using slow start mode gives targets time to warm up before the load balancer sends them a full share of requests. After you enable slow start for a target group, targets enter slow start mode when they are registered with the target group and exit slow start mode when the configured slow start duration period elapses. The load balancer linearly increases the number of requests that it can send to a target in slow start mode. After a target exits slow start mode, the load balancer can send it a full share of requests.

Considerations

- When you enable slow start for a target group, the targets already registered with the target group do not enter slow start mode.
- When you enable slow start for an empty target group and then register one or more targets using a single registration operation, these targets do not enter slow start mode. Newly registered targets enter slow start mode only when there is at least one registered target that is not in slow start mode.
- If you deregister a target in slow start mode, the target exits slow start mode. If you register the same target again, it enters slow start mode again.
- If a target in slow start mode becomes unhealthy and then healthy again before the duration period elapses, the target remains in slow start mode and exits slow start mode when the remainder of the duration period

elapses. If a target that is not in slow start mode changes from unhealthy to healthy, it does not enter slow start mode.

To update the slow start duration value using the console

1. Open the Amazon EC2 console at https://console.aws.amazon.com/ec2/.

2. On the navigation pane, under **LOAD BALANCING**, choose **Target Groups**.

3. Select the target group. The current value is displayed on the **Description** tab as **Slow start duration**.

4. On the **Description** tab, choose **Edit attributes**.

5. On the **Edit attributes** page, change the value of **Slow start duration** as needed, and then choose **Save**. To disable slow start mode, set the duration to 0.

To update the slow start duration value using the AWS CLI
Use the modify-target-group-attributes command with the `slow_start.duration_seconds` attribute.

Sticky Sessions

Sticky sessions are a mechanism to route requests to the same target in a target group. This is useful for servers that maintain state information in order to provide a continuous experience to clients. To use sticky sessions, the clients must support cookies.

When a load balancer first receives a request from a client, it routes the request to a target and generates a cookie to include in the response to the client. The next request from that client contains the cookie. If sticky sessions are enabled for the target group and the request goes to the same target group, the load balancer detects the cookie and routes the request to the same target.

Application Load Balancers support load balancer-generated cookies only. The name of the cookie is AWSALB. The contents of these cookies are encrypted using a rotating key. You cannot decrypt or modify load balancer-generated cookies.

WebSockets connections are inherently sticky. If the client requests a connection upgrade to WebSockets, the target that returns an HTTP 101 status code to accept the connection upgrade is the target used in the WebSockets connection. After the WebSockets upgrade is complete, cookie-based stickiness is not used.

You enable sticky sessions at the target group level. You can also set the duration for the stickiness of the load balancer-generated cookie, in seconds. The duration is set with each request. Therefore, if the client sends a request before each duration period expires, the sticky session continues. If you enable sticky sessions on multiple target groups, we recommend that you configure the same duration for all target groups.

To enable sticky sessions using the console

1. Open the Amazon EC2 console at https://console.aws.amazon.com/ec2/.

2. On the navigation pane, under **LOAD BALANCING**, choose **Target Groups**.

3. Select the target group.

4. On the **Description** tab, choose **Edit attributes**.

5. On the **Edit attributes** page, do the following:

    1. Select **Enable load balancer generated cookie stickiness**.

    2. For **Stickiness duration**, specify a value between 1 second and 7 days.

    3. Choose **Save**.

To enable sticky sessions using the AWS CLI
Use the modify-target-group-attributes command with the `stickiness.enabled` and `stickiness.lb_cookie.duration_seconds` attributes.

Create a Target Group

You register your targets with a target group. By default, the load balancer sends requests to registered targets using the port and protocol that you specified for the target group. You can override this port when you register each target with the target group.

After you create a target group, you can add tags.

To route traffic to the targets in a target group, specify the target group in an action when you create a listener or create a rule for your listener. For more information, see Listener Rules.

You can add or remove targets from your target group at any time. For more information, see Register Targets with Your Target Group. You can also modify the health check settings for your target group. For more information, see Modify the Health Check Settings of a Target Group.

To create a target group using the console

1. Open the Amazon EC2 console at https://console.aws.amazon.com/ec2/.

2. On the navigation pane, under **LOAD BALANCING**, choose **Target Groups**.

3. Choose **Create target group**.

4. For **Target group name**, type a name for the target group.

5. (Optional) For **Protocol** and **Port**, modify the default values as needed.

6. For **Target type**, select `instance` to specify targets by instance ID or `ip` to specify targets by IP address.

7. For **VPC**, select a virtual private cloud (VPC).

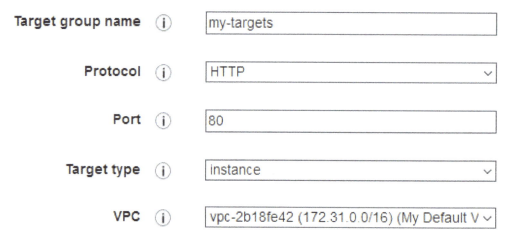

8. (Optional) For **Health check settings** and **Advanced health check settings**, modify the default settings as needed.

9. Choose **Create**.

10. (Optional) Add one or more tags as follows:

    1. Select the newly created target group.

    2. On the **Tags** tab, choose **Add/Edit Tags**.

    3. On the **Add/Edit Tags** page, for each tag you add, choose **Create Tag** and then specify the tag key and tag value. When you have finished adding tags, choose **Save**.

11. (Optional) To add targets to the target group, see Register Targets with Your Target Group.

To create a target group using the AWS CLI

Use the create-target-group command to create the target group, the add-tags command to tag your target group, and the register-targets command to add targets.

Health Checks for Your Target Groups

Your Application Load Balancer periodically sends requests to its registered targets to test their status. These tests are called *health checks*.

Each load balancer node routes requests only to the healthy targets in the enabled Availability Zones for the load balancer. Each load balancer node checks the health of each target, using the health check settings for the target group with which the target is registered. After your target is registered, it must pass one health check to be considered healthy. After each health check is completed, the load balancer node closes the connection that was established for the health check.

If no Availability Zone contains a healthy target, the load balancer nodes route requests to all targets.

Health checks do not support WebSockets.

Health Check Settings

You configure health checks for the targets in a target group using the following settings. The load balancer sends a health check request to each registered target every **HealthCheckIntervalSeconds** seconds, using the specified port, protocol, and ping path. It waits for the target to respond within the response timeout period. If the health checks exceed the threshold for consecutive failed responses, the load balancer takes the target out of service. When the health checks exceed the threshold for consecutive successful responses, the load balancer puts the target back in service.

Setting	Description
HealthCheckProtocol	The protocol the load balancer uses when performing health checks on targets. The possible protocols are HTTP and HTTPS. The default is the HTTP protocol.
HealthCheckPort	The port the load balancer uses when performing health checks on targets. The default is to use the port on which each target receives traffic from the load balancer.
HealthCheckPath	The ping path that is the destination on the targets for health checks. The default is /.
HealthCheckTimeoutSeconds	The amount of time, in seconds, during which no response from a target means a failed health check. The range is 2–60 seconds. The default is 5 seconds.
HealthCheckIntervalSeconds	The approximate amount of time, in seconds, between health checks of an individual target. The range is 5–300 seconds. The default is 30 seconds.
HealthyThresholdCount	The number of consecutive successful health checks required before considering an unhealthy target healthy. The range is 2–10. The default is 5.
UnhealthyThresholdCount	The number of consecutive failed health checks required before considering a target unhealthy. The range is 2–10. The default is 2.

Setting	Description
Matcher	The HTTP codes to use when checking for a successful response from a target. You can specify values or ranges of values between 200 and 499. The default value is 200.

Target Health Status

Before the load balancer sends a health check request to a target, you must register it with a target group, specify its target group in a listener rule, and ensure that the Availability Zone of the target is enabled for the load balancer. Before a target can receive requests from the load balancer, it must pass the initial health checks. After a target passes the initial health checks, its status is `Healthy`.

The following table describes the possible values for the health status of a registered target.

Value	Description
`initial`	The load balancer is in the process of registering the target or performing the initial health checks on the target.
`healthy`	The target is healthy.
`unhealthy`	The target did not respond to a health check or failed the health check.
`unused`	The target is not registered with a target group, the target group is not used in a listener rule for the load balancer, or the target is in an Availability Zone that is not enabled for the load balancer.
`draining`	The target is deregistering and connection draining is in process.

Health Check Reason Codes

If the status of a target is any value other than `Healthy`, the API returns a reason code and a description of the issue, and the console displays the same description in a tooltip. Reason codes that begin with `Elb` originate on the load balancer side and reason codes that begin with `Target` originate on the target side.

Reason code	Description
`Elb.InitialHealthChecking`	Initial health checks in progress
`Elb.InternalError`	Health checks failed due to an internal error
`Elb.RegistrationInProgress`	Target registration is in progress
`Target.DeregistrationInProgress`	Target deregistration is in progress
`Target.FailedHealthChecks`	Health checks failed
`Target.InvalidState`	Target is in the stopped state Target is in the terminated state Target is in the terminated or stopped state Target is in an invalid state
`Target.IpUnusable`	The IP address cannot be used as a target, as it is in use by a load balancer.
`Target.NotInUse`	Target group is not configured to receive traffic from the load balancer Target is in an Availability Zone that is not enabled for the load balancer

Reason code	Description
Target.NotRegistered	Target is not registered to the target group
Target.ResponseCodeMismatch	Health checks failed with these codes: [*code*]
Target.Timeout	Request timed out

Check the Health of Your Targets

You can check the health status of the targets registered with your target groups.

To check the health of your targets using the console

1. Open the Amazon EC2 console at https://console.aws.amazon.com/ec2/.

2. On the navigation pane, under **LOAD BALANCING**, choose **Target Groups**.

3. Select the target group.

4. On the **Targets** tab, the **Status** column indicates the status of each target.

5. If the status is any value other than `Healthy`, view the tooltip for more information.

To check the health of your targets using the AWS CLI
Use the describe-target-health command. The output of this command contains the target health state. If the status is any value other than `Healthy`, the output also includes a reason code.

Modify the Health Check Settings of a Target Group

You can modify the health check settings for your target group at any time.

To modify the health check settings of a target group using the console

1. Open the Amazon EC2 console at https://console.aws.amazon.com/ec2/.

2. On the navigation pane, under **LOAD BALANCING**, choose **Target Groups**.

3. Select the target group.

4. On the **Health checks** tab, choose **Edit**.

5. On the **Edit target group** page, modify the settings as needed, and then choose **Save**.

To modify the health check settings of a target group using the AWS CLI
Use the modify-target-group command.

Register Targets with Your Target Group

You register your targets with a target group. You can register targets by instance ID or by IP address. For more information, see Target Groups for Your Application Load Balancers.

If demand on your currently registered targets increases, you can register additional targets in order to handle the demand. When your target is ready to handle requests, register it with your target group. The load balancer starts routing requests to the target as soon as the registration process completes and the target passes the initial health checks.

If demand on your registered targets decreases, or you need to service a target, you can deregister it from your target group. The load balancer stops routing requests to a target as soon as you deregister it. When the target is ready to receive requests, you can register it with the target group again.

When you deregister a target, the load balancer waits until in-flight requests have completed. This is known as *connection draining*. The status of a target is `draining` while connection draining is in progress.

When you deregister a target that was registered by IP address, you must wait for the deregistration delay to complete before you can register the same IP address again.

If you are registering targets by instance ID, you can use your load balancer with an Auto Scaling group. After you attach a target group to an Auto Scaling group and the group scales out, the instances launched by the Auto Scaling group are automatically registered with the target group. If you detach the target group from the Auto Scaling group, the instances are automatically deregistered from the target group. For more information, see Attaching a Load Balancer to Your Auto Scaling Group in the *Amazon EC2 Auto Scaling User Guide*.

Target Security Groups

When you register EC2 instances as targets, you must ensure that the security groups for your instances allow the load balancer to communicate with your instances on both the listener port and the health check port.

Recommended Rules

Inbound
Source
load balancer security group
load balancer security group

We also recommend that you allow inbound ICMP traffic to support Path MTU Discovery. For more information, see Path MTU Discovery in the *Amazon EC2 User Guide for Linux Instances*.

Register or Deregister Targets

When you create a target group, you specify whether you must register targets by instance ID or IP address.

Topics

- Register or Deregister Targets by Instance ID
- Register or Deregister Targets by IP Address

Register or Deregister Targets by Instance ID

The instance must be in the virtual private cloud (VPC) that you specified for the target group. The instance must also be in the `running` state when you register it.

To register or deregister targets by instance ID using the console

1. Open the Amazon EC2 console at https://console.aws.amazon.com/ec2/.

2. On the navigation pane, under **LOAD BALANCING**, choose **Target Groups**.

3. Select your target group.

4. On the **Targets** tab, choose **Edit**.

5. To register instances, select them from **Instances**, modify the default instance port as needed, and choose **Add to registered**.

6. To deregister instances, select them from **Registered instances** and choose **Remove**.

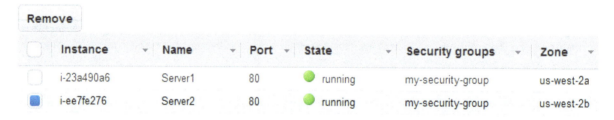

7. Choose **Save**.

To register or deregister targets using the AWS CLI
Use the register-targets command to add targets and the deregister-targets command to remove targets.

Register or Deregister Targets by IP Address

The IP addresses that you register must be from the subnets of the VPC for the target group, the RFC 1918 range (10.0.0.0/8, 172.16.0.0/12, and 192.168.0.0/16), and the RFC 6598 range (100.64.0.0/10). You cannot register publicly routable IP addresses.

To register or deregister targets by IP address using the console

1. Open the Amazon EC2 console at https://console.aws.amazon.com/ec2/.

2. On the navigation pane, under **LOAD BALANCING**, choose **Target Groups**.

3. Select your target group.

4. On the **Targets** tab, choose **Edit**.

5. To register IP addresses, choose the **Register targets** icon (the plus sign) in the menu bar. For each IP address, select the network, type the IP address and port, and choose **Add to list**. When you are finished specifying addresses, choose **Register**.

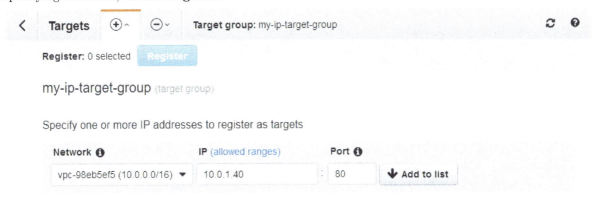

6. To deregister IP addresses, choose the **Deregister targets** icon (the minus sign) in the menu bar. If you have many registered IP addresses, you might find it helpful to add a filter or change the sort order. Select the IP addresses and then choose **Deregister**.

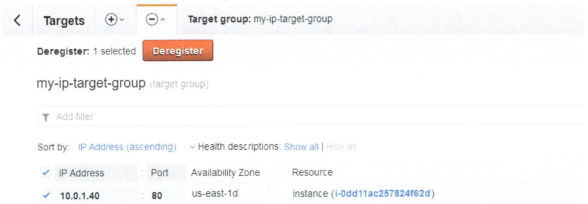

7. To leave this screen, choose the **Back to target group** icon (the back button) in the menu bar.

To register or deregister targets using the AWS CLI
Use the register-targets command to add targets and the deregister-targets command to remove targets.

Tags for Your Target Group

Tags help you to categorize your target groups in different ways, for example, by purpose, owner, or environment.

You can add multiple tags to each target group. Tag keys must be unique for each target group. If you add a tag with a key that is already associated with the target group, it updates the value of that tag.

When you are finished with a tag, you can remove it.

Restrictions

- Maximum number of tags per resource—50
- Maximum key length—127 Unicode characters
- Maximum value length—255 Unicode characters
- Tag keys and values are case-sensitive. Allowed characters are letters, spaces, and numbers representable in UTF-8, plus the following special characters: + - = . _ : / @. Do not use leading or trailing spaces.
- Do not use the `aws:` prefix in your tag names or values because it is reserved for AWS use. You can't edit or delete tag names or values with this prefix. Tags with this prefix do not count against your tags per resource limit.

To update the tags for a target group using the console

1. Open the Amazon EC2 console at https://console.aws.amazon.com/ec2/.

2. On the navigation pane, under **LOAD BALANCING**, choose **Target Groups**.

3. Select the target group.

4. On the **Tags** tab, choose **Add/Edit Tags** and do one or more of the following:

    1. To update a tag, edit the values of **Key** and **Value**.

    2. To add a new tag, choose **Create Tag** and type values for **Key** and **Value**.

    3. To delete a tag, choose the delete icon (X) next to the tag.

5. When you have finished updating tags, choose **Save**.

To update the tags for a target group using the AWS CLI
Use the add-tags and remove-tags commands.

Delete a Target Group

If a target group is not referenced by any actions, you can delete it. Deleting a target group does not affect the targets registered with the target group. If you no longer need a registered EC2 instance, you can stop or terminate it.

To delete a target group using the console

1. Open the Amazon EC2 console at https://console.aws.amazon.com/ec2/.

2. On the navigation pane, under **LOAD BALANCING**, choose **Target Groups**.

3. Select the target group and choose **Actions**, **Delete**.

4. When prompted for confirmation, choose **Yes**.

To delete a target group using the AWS CLI
Use the delete-target-group command.

Monitor Your Application Load Balancers

You can use the following features to monitor your load balancers, analyze traffic patterns, and troubleshoot issues with your load balancers and targets.

CloudWatch metrics
You can use Amazon CloudWatch to retrieve statistics about data points for your load balancers and targets as an ordered set of time-series data, known as *metrics*. You can use these metrics to verify that your system is performing as expected. For more information, see CloudWatch Metrics for Your Application Load Balancer.

Access logs
You can use access logs to capture detailed information about the requests made to your load balancer and store them as log files in Amazon S3. You can use these access logs to analyze traffic patterns and to troubleshoot issues with your targets. For more information, see Access Logs for Your Application Load Balancer.

Request tracing
You can use request tracing to track HTTP requests. The load balancer adds a header with a trace identifier to each request it receives. For more information, see Request Tracing for Your Application Load Balancer.

CloudTrail logs
You can use AWS CloudTrail to capture detailed information about the calls made to the Elastic Load Balancing API and store them as log files in Amazon S3. You can use these CloudTrail logs to determine which calls were made, the source IP address where the call came from, who made the call, when the call was made, and so on. For more information, see AWS CloudTrail Logging for Your Application Load Balancer.

CloudWatch Metrics for Your Application Load Balancer

Elastic Load Balancing publishes data points to Amazon CloudWatch for your load balancers and your targets. CloudWatch enables you to retrieve statistics about those data points as an ordered set of time-series data, known as *metrics*. Think of a metric as a variable to monitor, and the data points as the values of that variable over time. For example, you can monitor the total number of healthy targets for a load balancer over a specified time period. Each data point has an associated time stamp and an optional unit of measurement.

You can use metrics to verify that your system is performing as expected. For example, you can create a CloudWatch alarm to monitor a specified metric and initiate an action (such as sending a notification to an email address) if the metric goes outside what you consider an acceptable range.

Elastic Load Balancing reports metrics to CloudWatch only when requests are flowing through the load balancer. If there are requests flowing through the load balancer, Elastic Load Balancing measures and sends its metrics in 60-second intervals. If there are no requests flowing through the load balancer or no data for a metric, the metric is not reported.

For more information, see the Amazon CloudWatch User Guide.

Topics

- Application Load Balancer Metrics
- Metric Dimensions for Application Load Balancers
- Statistics for Application Load Balancer Metrics
- View CloudWatch Metrics for Your Load Balancer

Application Load Balancer Metrics

The `AWS/ApplicationELB` namespace includes the following metrics for load balancers.

Metric	Description
ActiveConnectionCount	The total number of concurrent TCP connections active from clients to the load balancer and from the load balancer to targets. **Reporting criteria**: There is a nonzero value **Statistics**: The most useful statistic is Sum. [See the AWS documentation website for more details]
ClientTLSNegotiationErrorCount	The number of TLS connections initiated by the client that did not establish a session with the load balancer. Possible causes include a mismatch of ciphers or protocols. **Reporting criteria**: There is a nonzero value **Statistics**: The most useful statistic is Sum. [See the AWS documentation website for more details]
ConsumedLCUs	The number of load balancer capacity units (LCU) used by your load balancer. You pay for the number of LCUs that you use per hour. For more information, see Elastic Load Balancing Pricing. **Reporting criteria**: Always reported **Statistics**: All [See the AWS documentation website for more details]

Metric	Description
HTTPCode_ELB_4XX_Count	The number of HTTP 4XX client error codes that originate from the load balancer. Client errors are generated when requests are malformed or incomplete. These requests have not been received by the target. This count does not include any response codes generated by the targets. **Reporting criteria**: There is a nonzero value **Statistics**: The most useful statistic is Sum. Note that Minimum, Maximum, and Average all return 1. [See the AWS documentation website for more details]
HTTPCode_ELB_5XX_Count	The number of HTTP 5XX server error codes that originate from the load balancer. This count does not include any response codes generated by the targets. **Reporting criteria**: There is a nonzero value **Statistics**: The most useful statistic is Sum. Note that Minimum, Maximum, and Average all return 1. [See the AWS documentation website for more details]
IPv6ProcessedBytes	The total number of bytes processed by the load balancer over IPv6. **Reporting criteria**: There is a nonzero value **Statistics**: The most useful statistic is Sum. [See the AWS documentation website for more details]
IPv6RequestCount	The number of IPv6 requests received by the load balancer. **Reporting criteria**: There is a nonzero value **Statistics**: The most useful statistic is Sum. Note that Minimum, Maximum, and Average all return 1. [See the AWS documentation website for more details]
NewConnectionCount	The total number of new TCP connections established from clients to the load balancer and from the load balancer to targets. **Reporting criteria**: There is a nonzero value **Statistics**: The most useful statistic is Sum. [See the AWS documentation website for more details]
ProcessedBytes	The total number of bytes processed by the load balancer over IPv4 and IPv6. **Reporting criteria**: There is a nonzero value **Statistics**: The most useful statistic is Sum. [See the AWS documentation website for more details]
RejectedConnectionCount	The number of connections that were rejected because the load balancer had reached its maximum number of connections. **Reporting criteria**: There is a nonzero value **Statistics**: The most useful statistic is Sum. [See the AWS documentation website for more details]

Metric	Description
RequestCount	The number of requests processed over IPv4 and IPv6. This count includes only the requests with a response generated by a target of the load balancer. **Reporting criteria**: Always reported **Statistics**: The most useful statistic is Sum. [See the AWS documentation website for more details]
RuleEvaluations	The number of rules processed by the load balancer given a request rate averaged over an hour. **Reporting criteria**: There is a nonzero value **Statistics**: The most useful statistic is Sum. [See the AWS documentation website for more details]

The `AWS/ApplicationELB` namespace includes the following metrics for targets.

Metric	Description
HealthyHostCount	The number of targets that are considered healthy. **Reporting criteria**: Always reported **Statistics**: The most useful statistics are Average, Minimum, and Maximum. [See the AWS documentation website for more details]
HTTPCode_Target_2XX_Count, HTTP-Code_Target_3XX_Count, HTTP-Code_Target_4XX_Count, HTTP-Code_Target_5XX_Count	The number of HTTP response codes generated by the targets. This does not include any response codes generated by the load balancer. **Reporting criteria**: There is a nonzero value **Statistics**: The most useful statistic is Sum. Note that Minimum, Maximum, and Average all return 1. [See the AWS documentation website for more details]
RequestCountPerTarget	The average number of requests received by each target in a target group. You must specify the target group using the TargetGroup dimension. **Reporting criteria**: There is a nonzero value **Statistics**: The only valid statistic is Sum. Note that this represents the average not the sum. [See the AWS documentation website for more details]
TargetConnectionErrorCount	The number of connections that were not successfully established between the load balancer and target. **Reporting criteria**: There is a nonzero value **Statistics**: The most useful statistic is Sum. [See the AWS documentation website for more details]

Metric	Description
TargetResponseTime	The time elapsed, in seconds, after the request leaves the load balancer until a response from the target is received. This is equivalent to the `target_processing_time` field in the access logs. **Reporting criteria**: There is a nonzero value **Statistics**: The most useful statistics are `Average` and `pNN.NN` (percentiles). [See the AWS documentation website for more details]
TargetTLSNegotiationErrorCount	The number of TLS connections initiated by the load balancer that did not establish a session with the target. Possible causes include a mismatch of ciphers or protocols. **Reporting criteria**: There is a nonzero value **Statistics**: The most useful statistic is `Sum`. [See the AWS documentation website for more details]
UnHealthyHostCount	The number of targets that are considered unhealthy. **Reporting criteria**: Always reported **Statistics**: The most useful statistics are `Average`, `Minimum`, and `Maximum`. [See the AWS documentation website for more details]

The `AWS/ApplicationELB` namespace includes the following metrics for user authentication.

Metric	Description
ELBAuthError	The number of user authentications that could not be completed because an authenticate action was misconfigured, the load balancer couldn't establish a connection with the IdP, or the load balancer couldn't complete the authentication flow due to an internal error. **Reporting criteria**: There is a nonzero value **Statistics**: The only meaningful statistic is `Sum`. **Dimensions**: `LoadBalancer`
ELBAuthFailure	The number of user authentications that could not be completed because the IdP denied access to the user or an authorization code was used more than once. **Reporting criteria**: There is a nonzero value **Statistics**: The only meaningful statistic is `Sum`. **Dimensions**: `LoadBalancer`
ELBAuthLatency	The time elapsed, in milliseconds, to query the IdP for the ID token and user info. If one or more of these operations fail, this is the time to failure. **Reporting criteria**: There is a nonzero value **Statistics**: All statistics are meaningful. **Dimensions**: `LoadBalancer`

Metric	Description
ELBAuthSuccess	The number of authenticate actions that were successful. This metric is incremented at the end of the authentication workflow, after the load balancer has retrieved the user claims from the IdP. **Reporting criteria:** There is a nonzero value **Statistics:** The most useful statistic is Sum. **Dimensions:** `LoadBalancer`

Metric Dimensions for Application Load Balancers

To filter the metrics for your Application Load Balancer, use the following dimensions.

Dimension	Description
AvailabilityZone	Filter the metric data by Availability Zone.
LoadBalancer	Filter the metric data by load balancer. Specify the load balancer as follows: app/*load-balancer-name*/*1234567890123456* (the final portion of the load balancer ARN).
TargetGroup	Filter the metric data by target group. Specify the target group as follows: targetgroup/*target-group-name*/*1234567890123456* (the final portion of the target group ARN).

Statistics for Application Load Balancer Metrics

CloudWatch provides statistics based on the metric data points published by Elastic Load Balancing. Statistics are metric data aggregations over specified period of time. When you request statistics, the returned data stream is identified by the metric name and dimension. A dimension is a name/value pair that uniquely identifies a metric. For example, you can request statistics for all the healthy EC2 instances behind a load balancer launched in a specific Availability Zone.

The `Minimum` and `Maximum` statistics reflect the minimum and maximum reported by the individual load balancer nodes. For example, suppose there are 2 load balancer nodes. One node has `HealthyHostCount` with a `Minimum` of 2, a `Maximum` of 10, and an `Average` of 6, while the other node has `HealthyHostCount` with a `Minimum` of 1, a `Maximum` of 5, and an `Average` of 3. Therefore, the load balancer has a `Minimum` of 1, a `Maximum` of 10, and an `Average` of about 4.

The `Sum` statistic is the aggregate value across all load balancer nodes. Because metrics include multiple reports per period, `Sum` is only applicable to metrics that are aggregated across all load balancer nodes.

The `SampleCount` statistic is the number of samples measured. Because metrics are gathered based on sampling intervals and events, this statistic is typically not useful. For example, with `HealthyHostCount`, `SampleCount` is based on the number of samples that each load balancer node reports, not the number of healthy hosts.

A percentile indicates the relative standing of a value in a data set. You can specify any percentile, using up to two decimal places (for example, p95.45). For example, the 95th percentile means that 95 percent of the data is below this value and 5 percent is above. Percentiles are often used to isolate anomalies. For example, suppose that an application serves the majority of requests from a cache in 1-2 ms, but in 100-200 ms if the cache is empty. The maximum reflects the slowest case, around 200 ms. The average doesn't indicate the distribution of the data. Percentiles provide a more meaningful view of the application's performance. By using the 99th percentile as an Auto Scaling trigger or a CloudWatch alarm, you can target that no more than 1 percent of requests take longer than 2 ms to process.

View CloudWatch Metrics for Your Load Balancer

You can view the CloudWatch metrics for your load balancers using the Amazon EC2 console. These metrics are displayed as monitoring graphs. The monitoring graphs show data points if the load balancer is active and receiving requests.

Alternatively, you can view metrics for your load balancer using the CloudWatch console.

To view metrics using the Amazon EC2 console

1. Open the Amazon EC2 console at https://console.aws.amazon.com/ec2/.

2. To view metrics filtered by target group, do the following:

   1. In the navigation pane, choose **Target Groups**.

   2. Select your target group, and then choose the **Monitoring** tab.

   3. (Optional) To filter the results by time, select a time range from **Showing data for**.

   4. To get a larger view of a single metric, select its graph.

3. To view metrics filtered by load balancer, do the following:

   1. In the navigation pane, choose **Load Balancers**.

   2. Select your load balancer, and then choose the **Monitoring** tab.

   3. (Optional) To filter the results by time, select a time range from **Showing data for**.

   4. To get a larger view of a single metric, select its graph.

To view metrics using the CloudWatch console

1. Open the CloudWatch console at https://console.aws.amazon.com/cloudwatch/.

2. In the navigation pane, choose **Metrics**.

3. Select the **ApplicationELB** namespace.

4. (Optional) To view a metric across all dimensions, type its name in the search field.

5. (Optional) To filter by dimension, select one of the following:

   - To display only the metrics reported for your load balancers, choose **Per AppELB Metrics**. To view the metrics for a single load balancer, type its name in the search field.
   - To display only the metrics reported for your target groups, choose **Per AppELB, per TG Metrics**. To view the metrics for a single target group, type its name in the search field.
   - To display only the metrics reported for your load balancers by Availability Zone, choose **Per AppELB, per AZ Metrics**. To view the metrics for a single load balancer, type its name in the search field. To view the metrics for a single Availability Zone, type its name in the search field.
   - To display only the metrics reported for your load balancers by Availability Zone and target group, choose **Per AppELB, per AZ, per TG Metrics**. To view the metrics for a single load balancer, type its name in the search field. To view the metrics for a single target group, type its name in the search field. To view the metrics for a single Availability Zone, type its name in the search field.

To view metrics using the AWS CLI
Use the following list-metrics command to list the available metrics:

```
1 aws cloudwatch list-metrics --namespace AWS/ApplicationELB
```

To get the statistics for a metric using the AWS CLI

Use the following get-metric-statistics command get statistics for the specified metric and dimension. Note that CloudWatch treats each unique combination of dimensions as a separate metric. You can't retrieve statistics using combinations of dimensions that were not specially published. You must specify the same dimensions that were used when the metrics were created.

```
1 aws cloudwatch get-metric-statistics --namespace AWS/ApplicationELB \
2 --metric-name UnHealthyHostCount --statistics Average  --period 3600 \
3 --dimensions Name=LoadBalancer,Value=app/my-load-balancer/50dc6c495c0c9188 \
4 Name=TargetGroup,Value=targetgroup/my-targets/73e2d6bc24d8a067 \
5 --start-time 2016-04-18T00:00:00Z --end-time 2016-04-21T00:00:00Z
```

The following is example output:

```
1 {
2     "Datapoints": [
3         {
4             "Timestamp": "2016-04-18T22:00:00Z",
5             "Average": 0.0,
6             "Unit": "Count"
7         },
8         {
9             "Timestamp": "2016-04-18T04:00:00Z",
10            "Average": 0.0,
11            "Unit": "Count"
12        },
13        ...
14    ],
15    "Label": "UnHealthyHostCount"
16 }
```

Access Logs for Your Application Load Balancer

Elastic Load Balancing provides access logs that capture detailed information about requests sent to your load balancer. Each log contains information such as the time the request was received, the client's IP address, latencies, request paths, and server responses. You can use these access logs to analyze traffic patterns and troubleshoot issues.

Access logging is an optional feature of Elastic Load Balancing that is disabled by default. After you enable access logging for your load balancer, Elastic Load Balancing captures the logs and stores them in the Amazon S3 bucket that you specify as compressed files. You can disable access logging at any time.

Elastic Load Balancing supports server-side encryption for access logs for your Application Load Balancer. This protects the log data stored in your S3 bucket and meets compliance requirements for data at rest. Each access log file is automatically encrypted before it is stored in your S3 bucket and decrypted when you access it. You do not need to take any action as there is no difference in the way you access encrypted or unencrypted log files. Each log file is encrypted with a unique key employing strong multi-factor encryption. As an additional safeguard, the key itself encrypted with a master key that is regularly rotated. For more information, see Protecting Data Using Server-Side Encryption with Amazon S3-Managed Encryption Keys (SSE-S3) in the *Amazon Simple Storage Service Developer Guide*.

There is no additional charge for access logs. You are charged storage costs for Amazon S3, but not charged for the bandwidth used by Elastic Load Balancing to send log files to Amazon S3. For more information about storage costs, see Amazon S3 Pricing.

Topics

- Access Log Files
- Access Log Entries
- Bucket Permissions
- Enable Access Logging
- Disable Access Logging
- Processing Access Log Files

Access Log Files

Elastic Load Balancing publishes a log file for each load balancer node every 5 minutes. Log delivery is eventually consistent. The load balancer can deliver multiple logs for the same period. This usually happens if the site has high traffic.

The file names of the access logs use the following format:

```
1  bucket[/prefix]/AWSLogs/aws-account-id/elasticloadbalancing/region/yyyy/mm/dd/aws-account-
       id_elasticloadbalancing_region_load-balancer-id_end-time_ip-address_random-string.log.gz
```

bucket
The name of the S3 bucket.

prefix
The prefix (logical hierarchy) in the bucket. If you don't specify a prefix, the logs are placed at the root level of the bucket.

aws-account-id
The AWS account ID of the owner.

region
The region for your load balancer and S3 bucket.

yyyy/mm/dd
The date that the log was delivered.

74

load-balancer-id

The resource ID of the load balancer. If the resource ID contains any forward slashes (/), they are replaced with periods (.).

end-time

The date and time that the logging interval ended. For example, an end time of 20140215T2340Z contains entries for requests made between 23:35 and 23:40.

ip-address

The IP address of the load balancer node that handled the request. For an internal load balancer, this is a private IP address.

random-string

A system-generated random string.

The following is an example log file name:

```
1  s3://my-bucket/prefix/AWSLogs/123456789012/elasticloadbalancing/us-east
       -2/2016/05/01/123456789012_elasticloadbalancing_us-east-2_my-loadbalancer_20140215T2340Z_172
       .160.001.192_20sg8hgm.log.gz
```

You can store your log files in your bucket for as long as you want, but you can also define Amazon S3 lifecycle rules to archive or delete log files automatically. For more information, see Object Lifecycle Management in the *Amazon Simple Storage Service Developer Guide.*

Access Log Entries

Elastic Load Balancing logs requests sent to the load balancer, including requests that never made it to the targets. For example, if a client sends a malformed request, or there are no healthy targets to respond to the request, the request is still logged. Note that Elastic Load Balancing does not log health check requests.

Each log entry contains the details of a single request (or connection in the case of WebSockets) made to the load balancer. For WebSockets, an entry is written only after the connection is closed. If the upgraded connection can't be established, the entry is the same as for an HTTP or HTTPS request.

Important

Elastic Load Balancing logs requests on a best-effort basis. We recommend that you use access logs to understand the nature of the requests, not as a complete accounting of all requests.

Syntax

The following table describes the fields of an access log entry, in order. All fields are delimited by spaces. When new fields are introduced, they are added to the end of the log entry. You should ignore any fields at the end of the log entry that you were not expecting.

Field	Description
type	The type of request or connection. The possible values are as follows (ignore any other values): [See the AWS documentation website for more details]
timestamp	The time when the load balancer generated a response to the client, in ISO 8601 format. For WebSockets, this is the time when the connection is closed.
elb	The resource ID of the load balancer. If you are parsing access log entries, note that resources IDs can contain forward slashes (/).

75

Field	Description
client:port	The IP address and port of the requesting client.
target:port	The IP address and port of the target that processed this request. If the client didn't send a full request, the load balancer can't dispatch the request to a target, and this value is set to -. If the request is blocked by AWS WAF, this value is set to - and the value of elb_status_code is set to 403.
request_processing_time	The total time elapsed, in seconds, from the time the load balancer received the request until the time it sent it to a target. This value is set to -1 if the load balancer can't dispatch the request to a target. This can happen if the target closes the connection before the idle timeout or if the client sends a malformed request.
target_processing_time	The total time elapsed, in seconds, from the time the load balancer sent the request to a target until the target started to send the response headers. This value is set to -1 if the load balancer can't dispatch the request to a target. This can happen if the target closes the connection before the idle timeout or if the client sends a malformed request.
response_processing_time	The total time elapsed (in seconds) from the time the load balancer received the response header from the target until it started to send the response to the client. This includes both the queuing time at the load balancer and the connection acquisition time from the load balancer to the client. This value is set to -1 if the load balancer can't send the request to a target. This can happen if the target closes the connection before the idle timeout or if the client sends a malformed request.
elb_status_code	The status code of the response from the load balancer.
target_status_code	The status code of the response from the target. This value is recorded only if a connection was established to the target and the target sent a response. Otherwise, the value is set to -.
received_bytes	The size of the request, in bytes, received from the client (requester). For HTTP requests, this includes the headers. For WebSockets, this is the total number of bytes received from the client on the connection.
sent_bytes	The size of the response, in bytes, sent to the client (requester). For HTTP requests, this includes the headers. For WebSockets, this is the total number of bytes sent to the client on the connection.

Field	Description
request	The request line from the client enclosed in double quotes and logged using the following format: HTTP method + protocol://host:port/uri + HTTP version.
user_agent	A User-Agent string that identifies the client that originated the request. The string consists of one or more product identifiers, product[/version]. If the string is longer than 8 KB, it is truncated.
ssl_cipher	[HTTPS listener] The SSL cipher. This value is recorded only if the incoming connection was established after a successful negotiation. Otherwise, the value is set to -.
ssl_protocol	[HTTPS listener] The SSL protocol. This value is recorded only if the incoming connection was established after a successful negotiation. Otherwise, the value is set to -.
target_group_arn	The Amazon Resource Name (ARN) of the target group.
trace_id	The contents of the **X-Amzn-Trace-Id** header.
domain_name	[HTTPS listener] The SNI domain provided by the client during the TLS handshake. This value is set to - if the client doesn't support SNI or the domain doesn't match a certificate and the default certificate is presented to the client.
chosen_cert_arn	[HTTPS listener] The ARN of the certificate presented to the client.
matched_rule_priority	The priority value of the rule that matched the request. If a rule matched, this is a value from 1 to 50,000. If no rule matched and the default action was taken, the value is 0. If an error occurred, the value is -1.
request_creation_time	The time when the load balancer received the request from the client, in ISO 8601 format.
actions_executed	The actions taken when processing the request. This value is a comma-separated list with the following possible values: `waf`, `authenticate`, and `forward`. If no actions were taken, this value is set to -.

Examples

The following are example log entries. Note that the text appears on multiple lines only to make them easier to read.

Example HTTP Entry

The following is an example log entry for an HTTP listener (port 80 to port 80):

```
1  http 2016-08-10T22:08:42.945958Z app/my-loadbalancer/50dc6c495c0c9188
2  192.168.131.39:2817 10.0.0.1:80 0.000 0.001 0.000 200 200 34 366
3  "GET http://www.example.com:80/ HTTP/1.1" "curl/7.46.0" - -
```

```
4 arn:aws:elasticloadbalancing:us-east-2:123456789012:targetgroup/my-targets/73e2d6bc24d8a067
5 "Root=1-58337262-36d228ad5d99923122bbe354" - -
```

Example HTTPS Entry

The following is an example log entry for an HTTPS listener (port 443 to port 80):

```
1 https 2016-08-10T23:39:43.065466Z app/my-loadbalancer/50dc6c495c0c9188
2 192.168.131.39:2817 10.0.0.1:80 0.086 0.048 0.037 200 200 0 57
3 "GET https://www.example.com:443/ HTTP/1.1" "curl/7.46.0" ECDHE-RSA-AES128-GCM-SHA256 TLSv1.2
4 arn:aws:elasticloadbalancing:us-east-2:123456789012:targetgroup/my-targets/73e2d6bc24d8a067
5 "Root=1-58337281-1d84f3d73c47ec4e58577259" www.example.com arn:aws:acm:us-east-2:123456789012:
    certificate/12345678-1234-1234-1234-123456789012
```

Example HTTP/2 Entry

The following is an example log entry for an HTTP/2 stream.

```
1 h2 2016-08-10T00:10:33.145057Z app/my-loadbalancer/50dc6c495c0c9188
2 10.0.1.252:48160 10.0.0.66:9000 0.000 0.002 0.000 200 200 5 257
3 "GET https://10.0.2.105:773/ HTTP/2.0" "curl/7.46.0" ECDHE-RSA-AES128-GCM-SHA256 TLSv1.2
4 arn:aws:elasticloadbalancing:us-east-2:123456789012:targetgroup/my-targets/73e2d6bc24d8a067
5 "Root=1-58337327-72bd00b0343d75b906739c42" - -
```

Example WebSockets Entry

The following is an example log entry for a WebSockets connection.

```
1 ws 2016-08-10T00:32:08.923954Z app/my-loadbalancer/50dc6c495c0c9188
2 10.0.0.140:40914 10.0.1.192:8010 0.001 0.003 0.000 101 101 218 587
3 "GET http://10.0.0.30:80/ HTTP/1.1" "-" - -
4 arn:aws:elasticloadbalancing:us-east-2:123456789012:targetgroup/my-targets/73e2d6bc24d8a067
5 "Root=1-58337364-23a8c76965a2ef7629b185e3" - -
```

Example Secured WebSockets Entry

The following is an example log entry for a secured WebSockets connection.

```
1 wss 2016-08-10T00:42:46.423695Z app/my-loadbalancer/50dc6c495c0c9188
2 10.0.0.140:44244 10.0.0.171:8010 0.000 0.001 0.000 101 101 218 786
3 "GET https://10.0.0.30:443/ HTTP/1.1" "-" ECDHE-RSA-AES128-GCM-SHA256 TLSv1.2
4 arn:aws:elasticloadbalancing:us-west-2:123456789012:targetgroup/my-targets/73e2d6bc24d8a067
5 "Root=1-58337364-23a8c76965a2ef7629b185e3" - -
```

Bucket Permissions

When you enable access logging, you must specify an S3 bucket for the access logs. This bucket must be located in the same region as the load balancer, and must have a bucket policy that grants Elastic Load Balancing permission to write the access logs to your bucket. Bucket policies are a collection of JSON statements written in the access policy language to define access permissions for your bucket. Each statement includes information about a single permission and contains a series of elements.

Important

If you will use the console to enable access logging, you can skip to Enable Access Logging. If you will use the AWS CLI or an API to enable access logging, the bucket must exist and must have the required bucket policy.

If you need to create a bucket for your access logs, use the following procedure to create the bucket and add the required bucket policy. If you already have a bucket, start at step 4 to add or update the bucket policy for your bucket.

To create an Amazon S3 bucket with the required permissions

1. Open the Amazon S3 console at https://console.aws.amazon.com/s3/.

2. Choose **Create Bucket**.

3. In the **Create a Bucket** dialog box, do the following:

   1. For **Bucket Name**, enter a name for your bucket (for example, `my-loadbalancer-logs`). This name must be unique across all existing bucket names in Amazon S3. In some regions, there might be additional restrictions on bucket names. For more information, see Bucket Restrictions and Limitations in the *Amazon Simple Storage Service Developer Guide*.

   2. For **Region**, select the region where you created your load balancer.

   3. Choose **Create**.

4. Select the bucket and choose **Permissions**.

5. Choose **Bucket Policy**. If your bucket already has an attached policy, you can add the required statement to the existing policy.

6. Choose **Policy generator**. On the **AWS Policy Generator** page, do the following:

   1. For **Select Type of Policy**, choose **S3 Bucket Policy**.

   2. For **Effect**, choose **Allow**.

   3. For **Principal**, specify one of the following AWS account IDs to grant Elastic Load Balancing access to the S3 bucket. Use the account ID that corresponds to the region for your load balancer and bucket.
   [See the AWS documentation website for more details]

   * These regions requires a separate account. For more information, see AWS GovCloud (US) and China (Beijing).

   4. For **Actions**, choose `PutObject` to allow Elastic Load Balancing to store objects in the S3 bucket.

   5. For **Amazon Resource Name (ARN)**, enter the ARN of your S3 bucket in the following format. For *aws-account-id*, specify the ID of the AWS account that owns the load balancer (for example, *123456789012*).

   ```
   1 arn:aws:s3:::bucket/prefix/AWSLogs/aws-account-id/*
   ```

   Note that if you are using the `us-gov-west-1` region, specify `arn:aws-us-gov` instead of `arn:aws` in the ARN.

   6. Choose **Add Statement**, **Generate Policy**. The policy document should be similar to the following:

   ```
    1 {
    2   "Id": "Policy1429136655940",
    3   "Version": "2012-10-17",
    4   "Statement": [
    5     {
    6       "Sid": "Stmt1429136633762",
    7       "Action": [
    8         "s3:PutObject"
    9       ],
   10       "Effect": "Allow",
   11       "Resource": "arn:aws:s3:::my-loadbalancer-logs/my-app/AWSLogs/123456789012/*",
   12       "Principal": {
   13         "AWS": [
   14           "797873946194"
   15         ]
   16       }
   ```

```
17        }
18     ]
19 }
```

7. If you are creating a new bucket policy, copy the entire policy document, and then choose **Close**.

   If you are editing an existing bucket policy, copy the new statement from the policy document (the text between the [and] of the `Statement` element), and then choose **Close**.

7. Go back to the Amazon S3 console and paste the policy into the text area as appropriate.

8. Choose **Save**.

Enable Access Logging

When you enable access logging for your load balancer, you must specify the name of the S3 bucket where the load balancer will store the logs. The bucket must be in the same region as your load balancer, and must have a bucket policy that grants Elastic Load Balancing permission to write the access logs to the bucket. The bucket can be owned by a different account than the account that owns the load balancer.

To enable access logging using the console

1. Open the Amazon EC2 console at https://console.aws.amazon.com/ec2/.

2. In the navigation pane, choose **Load Balancers**.

3. Select your load balancer.

4. On the **Description** tab, choose **Edit attributes**.

5. On the **Edit load balancer attributes** page, do the following:

   1. Choose **Enable access logs**.

   2. For **S3 location**, type the name of your S3 bucket, including any prefix (for example, `my-loadbalancer-logs/my-app`). You can specify the name of an existing bucket or a name for a new bucket. If you specify an existing bucket, be sure that you own this bucket and that you configured the required bucket policy.

   3. (Optional) If the bucket does not exist, choose **Create this location for me**. You must specify a name that is unique across all existing bucket names in Amazon S3 and follows the DNS naming conventions. For more information, see Rules for Bucket Naming in the *Amazon Simple Storage Service Developer Guide*.

   4. Choose **Save**.

To enable access logging using the AWS CLI
Use the modify-load-balancer-attributes command.

To verify that Elastic Load Balancing created a test file in your S3 bucket

After access logging is enabled for your load balancer, Elastic Load Balancing validates the S3 bucket and creates a test file to ensure that the bucket policy specifies the required permissions. You can use the Amazon S3 console to verify that the test file was created. Note that the test file is not an actual access log file; it doesn't contain example records.

1. Open the Amazon S3 console at https://console.aws.amazon.com/s3/.

2. For **All Buckets**, select your S3 bucket.

3. Navigate to the test log file. The path should be as follows:

```
1 my-bucket/prefix/AWSLogs/123456789012/ELBAccessLogTestFile
```

To manage the S3 bucket for your access logs

After you enable access logging, be sure to disable access logging before you delete the bucket with your access logs. Otherwise, if there is a new bucket with the same name and the required bucket policy created in an AWS account that you don't own, Elastic Load Balancing could write the access logs for your load balancer to this new bucket.

Disable Access Logging

You can disable access logging for your load balancer at any time. After you disable access logging, your access logs remain in your S3 bucket until you delete the them. For more information, see Working with Buckets in the *Amazon Simple Storage Service Console User Guide*.

To disable access logging using the console

1. Open the Amazon EC2 console at https://console.aws.amazon.com/ec2/.

2. In the navigation pane, choose **Load Balancers**.

3. Select your load balancer.

4. On the **Description** tab, choose **Edit attributes**.

5. On the **Edit load balancer attributes** page, clear **Enable access logs**.

6. Choose **Save**.

To disable access logging using the AWS CLI

Use the modify-load-balancer-attributes command.

Processing Access Log Files

The access log files are compressed. If you open the files using the Amazon S3 console, they are uncompressed and the information is displayed. If you download the files, you must uncompress them to view the information.

If there is a lot of demand on your website, your load balancer can generate log files with gigabytes of data. You might not be able to process such a large amount of data using line-by-line processing. Therefore, you might have to use analytical tools that provide parallel processing solutions. For example, you can use the following analytical tools to analyze and process access logs:

- Amazon Athena is an interactive query service that makes it easy to analyze data in Amazon S3 using standard SQL. For more information, see Querying Application Load Balancer Logs in the *Amazon Athena User Guide*.
- Loggly
- Splunk
- Sumo Logic

Request Tracing for Your Application Load Balancer

You can use request tracing to track HTTP requests from clients to targets or other services. When the load balancer receives a request from a client, it adds or updates the **X-Amzn-Trace-Id** header before sending the request to the target. Any services or applications between the load balancer and the target can also add or update this header.

If you enable access logs, the contents of the **X-Amzn-Trace-Id** header are logged. For more information, see Access Logs for Your Application Load Balancer.

Syntax

The **X-Amzn-Trace-Id** header contains fields with the following format:

```
1 Field=version-time-id
```

Field
The name of the field. The supported values are `Root` and `Self`.
An application can add arbitrary fields for its own purposes. The load balancer preserves these fields but does not use them.

version
The version number.

time
The epoch time, in seconds.

id
The trace identifier.

Examples
If the **X-Amzn-Trace-Id** header is not present on an incoming request, the load balancer generates a header with a `Root` field and forwards the request. For example:

```
1 X-Amzn-Trace-Id: Root=1-67891233-abcdef012345678912345678
```

If the **X-Amzn-Trace-Id** header is present and has a `Root` field, the load balancer inserts a `Self` field and forwards the request. For example:

```
1 X-Amzn-Trace-Id: Self=1-67891234-12456789abcdef012345678;Root=1-67891233-
    abcdef012345678912345678
```

If an application adds a header with a `Root` field and a custom field, the load balancer preserves both fields, inserts a `Self` field, and forwards the request:

```
1 X-Amzn-Trace-Id: Self=1-67891234-12456789abcdef012345678;Root=1-67891233-
    abcdef012345678912345678;CalledFrom=app
```

If the **X-Amzn-Trace-Id** header is present and has a `Self` field, the load balancer updates the value of the `Self` field.

Limitations

- The load balancer updates the header when it receives an incoming request, not when it receives a response.
- If the HTTP headers are greater than 7 KB, the load balancer rewrites the **X-Amzn-Trace-Id** header with a `Root` field.
- With WebSockets, you can trace only until the upgrade request is successful.

AWS CloudTrail Logging for Your Application Load Balancer

Elastic Load Balancing is integrated with AWS CloudTrail, which captures API calls to AWS made by or on behalf of your AWS account, and delivers log files to an Amazon S3 bucket that you specify. There is no cost to use CloudTrail. However, the standard rates for Amazon S3 apply.

CloudTrail logs calls to the AWS APIs, including the Elastic Load Balancing API, whether you use them directly or indirectly through the AWS Management Console. You can use the information collected by CloudTrail to determine what API call was made, what source IP address was used, who made the call, when it was made, and so on.

To learn more about CloudTrail, including how to configure and enable it, see the AWS CloudTrail User Guide. For the complete list of Elastic Load Balancing API actions, see the Elastic Load Balancing API Reference version 2015-12-01.

To monitor other actions for your load balancer, such as when a client makes a request to your load balancer, use access logs. For more information, see Access Logs for Your Application Load Balancer.

Topics

- Enable CloudTrail Event Logging
- Elastic Load Balancing Event Records in CloudTrail Log Files

Enable CloudTrail Event Logging

If you haven't done so already, use the following steps to enable CloudTrail event logging for your account.

To enable CloudTrail event logging

1. Open the CloudTrail console at https://console.aws.amazon.com/cloudtrail/.

2. Choose **Get Started Now**.

3. For **Trail name**, type a name for your trail.

4. Leave **Apply trail to all regions** as **Yes**.

5. Choose an existing S3 bucket for your CloudTrail log files, or create a new one. To create a new bucket, type a unique name for **S3 bucket**. To use an existing bucket, change **Create a new S3 bucket** to **No** and then select your bucket from **S3 bucket**.

6. Choose **Turn on**.

The log files are written to your S3 bucket in the following location:

```
1  my-bucket/AWSLogs/123456789012/CloudTrail/region/yyyy/mm/dd/
```

For more information, see the AWS CloudTrail User Guide.

Elastic Load Balancing Event Records in CloudTrail Log Files

The log files from CloudTrail contain event information in JSON format. An event record represents a single AWS API call and includes information about the requested action, such as the user that requested the action, the date and the time of the request, the request parameter, and the response elements.

The log files include events for all AWS API calls for your AWS account, not just Elastic Load Balancing API calls. You can locate calls to the Elastic Load Balancing API by checking for `eventSource` elements with the value `elasticloadbalancing.amazonaws.com`. To view a record for a specific action, such as `CreateLoadBalancer`, check for `eventName` elements with the action name. To view records for calls made to the Amazon EC2 API by Elastic Load Balancing on your behalf, check for records with an `eventSource` element with the value `ec2.amazonaws.com` and an `invokedBy` element with the value `elasticloadbalancing.amazonaws.com`. For example, when your load balancer scales to handle a change in traffic volume, it calls the Amazon EC2 API to create and delete network interfaces.

The following example shows CloudTrail log records for a user who created a load balancer and then deleted it using the AWS CLI. You can identify the CLI using the `userAgent` elements. You can identify the requested API calls using the `eventName` elements. Information about the user (`Alice`) can be found in the `userIdentity` element. For more information about the different elements and values in a CloudTrail log file, see CloudTrail Event Reference in the *AWS CloudTrail User Guide*.

```
 1  {
 2      "Records": [
 3      . . .
 4      {
 5          "eventVersion: "1.03",
 6          "userIdentity": {
 7              "type": "IAMUser",
 8              "principalId": "123456789012",
 9              "arn": "arn:aws:iam::123456789012:user/Alice",
10              "accountId": "123456789012",
11              "accessKeyId": "AKIAIOSFODNN7EXAMPLE",
12              "userName": "Alice"
13          },
14          "eventTime": "2016-04-01T15:31:48Z",
15          "eventSource": "elasticloadbalancing.amazonaws.com",
16          "eventName": "CreateLoadBalancer",
17          "awsRegion": "us-west-2",
18          "sourceIPAddress": "198.51.100.1",
19          "userAgent": "aws-cli/1.10.10 Python/2.7.9 Windows/7 botocore/1.4.1",
20          "requestParameters": {
21              "subnets": ["subnet-8360a9e7","subnet-b7d581c0"],
22              "securityGroups": ["sg-5943793c"],
23              "name": "my-load-balancer",
24              "scheme": "internet-facing"
25          },
26          "responseElements": {
27              "loadBalancers":[{
28                  "type": "application",
29                  "loadBalancerName": "my-load-balancer",
30                  "vpcId": "vpc-3ac0fb5f",
31                  "securityGroups": ["sg-5943793c"],
32                  "state": {"code":"provisioning"},
33                  "availabilityZones": [
34                      {"subnetId":"subnet-8360a9e7","zoneName":"us-west-2a"},
35                      {"subnetId":"subnet-b7d581c0","zoneName":"us-west-2b"}
36                  ],
37                  "dNSName": "my-load-balancer-1836718677.us-west-2.elb.amazonaws.com",
38                  "canonicalHostedZoneId": "Z2P70J7HTTTPLU",
39                  "createdTime": "Apr 11, 2016 5:23:50 PM",
40                  "loadBalancerArn": "arn:aws:elasticloadbalancing:us-west-2:123456789012:loadbalancer
                      /app/my-load-balancer/ffcddace1759e1d0",
41                  "scheme": "internet-facing"
42              }]
43          },
44          "requestID": "b9960276-b9b2-11e3-8a13-f1ef1EXAMPLE",
45          "eventID": "6f4ab5bd-2daa-4d00-be14-d92efEXAMPLE",
```

```
46      "eventType": "AwsApiCall",
47      "apiVersion": "2015-12-01",
48      "recipientAccountId": "123456789012"
49    },
50    . . .
51    {
52      "eventVersion: "1.03",
53      "userIdentity": {
54        "type": "IAMUser",
55        "principalId": "123456789012",
56        "arn": "arn:aws:iam::123456789012:user/Alice",
57        "accountId": "123456789012",
58        "accessKeyId": "AKIAIOSFODNN7EXAMPLE",
59        "userName": "Alice"
60      },
61      "eventTime": "2016-04-01T15:31:48Z",
62      "eventSource": "elasticloadbalancing.amazonaws.com",
63      "eventName": "DeleteLoadBalancer",
64      "awsRegion": "us-west-2",
65      "sourceIPAddress": "198.51.100.1",
66      "userAgent": "aws-cli/1.10.10 Python/2.7.9 Windows/7 botocore/1.4.1",
67      "requestParameters": {
68        "loadBalancerArn": "arn:aws:elasticloadbalancing:us-west-2:123456789012:loadbalancer/
            app/my-load-balancer/ffcddace1759e1d0"
69      },
70      "responseElements": null,
71      "requestID": "349598b3-000e-11e6-a82b-298133eEXAMPLE",
72      "eventID": "75e81c95-4012-421f-a0cf-babdaEXAMPLE",
73      "eventType": "AwsApiCall",
74      "apiVersion": "2015-12-01",
75      "recipientAccountId": "123456789012"
76    },
77    . . .
78 ]}
```

You can also use one of the Amazon partner solutions that integrate with CloudTrail to read and analyze your CloudTrail log files. For more information, see the AWS CloudTrail Partners page.

Troubleshoot Your Application Load Balancers

The following information can help you troubleshoot issues with your Application Load Balancer.

Topics

- A registered target is not in service
- Clients cannot connect to an Internet-facing load balancer
- The load balancer sends requests to unhealthy targets
- The load balancer generates an HTTP error
- A target generates an HTTP error

A registered target is not in service

If a target is taking longer than expected to enter the `InService` state, it might be failing health checks. Your target is not in service until it passes one health check. For more information, see Health Checks for Your Target Groups.

Verify that your instance is failing health checks and then check for the following:

A security group does not allow traffic
The security group associated with an instance must allow traffic from the load balancer using the health check port and health check protocol. You can add a rule to the instance security group to allow all traffic from the load balancer security group. Also, the security group for your load balancer must allow traffic to the instances.

A network access control list (ACL) does not allow traffic
The network ACL associated with the subnets for your instances must allow inbound traffic on the health check port and outbound traffic on the ephemeral ports (1024-65535). The network ACL associated with the subnets for your load balancer nodes must allow inbound traffic on the ephemeral ports and outbound traffic on the health check and ephemeral ports.

The ping path does not exist
Create a target page for the health check and specify its path as the ping path.

The connection times out
First, verify that you can connect to the target directly from within the network using the private IP address of the target and the health check protocol. If you can't connect, check whether the instance is over-utilized, and add more targets to your target group if it is too busy to respond. If you can connect, it is possible that the target page is not responding before the health check timeout period. Choose a simpler target page for the health check or adjust the health check settings.

The target did not return a successful response code
By default, the success code is 200, but you can optionally specify additional success codes when you configure health checks. Confirm the success codes that the load balancer is expecting and that your application is configured to return these codes on success.

Clients cannot connect to an Internet-facing load balancer

If the load balancer is not responding to requests, check for the following:

Your Internet-facing load balancer is attached to a private subnet
Verify that you specified public subnets for your load balancer. A public subnet has a route to the Internet Gateway for your virtual private cloud (VPC).

A security group or network ACL does not allow traffic
The security group for the load balancer and any network ACLs for the load balancer subnets must allow inbound traffic from the clients and outbound traffic to the clients on the listener ports.

The load balancer sends requests to unhealthy targets

If there is at least one healthy registered target for your load balancer, the load balancer routes requests only to its healthy registered targets. If there are only unhealthy registered targets, the load balancer routes requests to all registered targets.

The load balancer generates an HTTP error

The following HTTP errors are generated by the load balancer. The load balancer sends the HTTP code to the client, saves the request to the access log, and increments the `HTTPCode_ELB_4XX_Count` or `HTTPCode_ELB_5XX_Count` metric.

Topics

- HTTP 400: Bad Request
- HTTP 401: Unauthorized
- HTTP 403: Forbidden
- HTTP 460
- HTTP 463
- HTTP 502: Bad Gateway
- HTTP 503: Service Unavailable
- HTTP 504: Gateway Timeout
- HTTP 561: Unauthorized

HTTP 400: Bad Request

Possible causes:

- The client sent a malformed request that does not meet the HTTP specification.
- The request header exceeded 16K per request line, 16K per single header, or 64K for the entire header.

HTTP 401: Unauthorized

You configured a listener rule to authenticate users. Either you configured `OnUnauthenticatedRequest` to deny unauthenticated users or the IdP denied access.

HTTP 403: Forbidden

You configured an AWS WAF web access control list (web ACL) to monitor requests to your Application Load Balancer and it blocked a request.

HTTP 460

The load balancer received a request from a client, but the client closed the connection with the load balancer before the idle timeout period elapsed.

Check whether the client timeout period is greater than the idle timeout period for the load balancer. Ensure that your target provides a response to the client before the client timeout period elapses, or increase the client timeout period to match the load balancer idle timeout, if the client supports this.

HTTP 463

The load balancer received an X-Forwarded-For request header with more than 30 IP addresses.

HTTP 502: Bad Gateway

Possible causes:

- The load balancer received a TCP RST from the target when attempting to establish a connection.
- The target closed the connection with a TCP RST or a TCP FIN while the load balancer had an outstanding request to the target. Check whether the keep-alive duration of the target is shorter than the idle timeout value of the load balancer.
- The target response is malformed or contains HTTP headers that are not valid.
- A new target group was used but no targets have passed an initial health check yet. A target must pass one health check to be considered healthy.
- The load balancer encountered an SSL handshake error or SSL handshake timeout (10 seconds) when connecting to a target.
- The deregistration delay period elapsed for a request being handled by a target that was deregistered. Increase the delay period so that lengthy operations can complete.

HTTP 503: Service Unavailable

The target groups for the load balancer have no registered targets.

HTTP 504: Gateway Timeout

Possible causes:

- The load balancer failed to establish a connection to the target before the connection timeout expired (10 seconds).
- The load balancer established a connection to the target but the target did not respond before the idle timeout period elapsed.
- The network ACL for the subnet did not allow traffic from the targets to the load balancer nodes on the ephemeral ports (1024-65535).
- The target returns a content-length header that is larger than the entity body. The load balancer timed out waiting for the missing bytes.

HTTP 561: Unauthorized

You configured a listener rule to authenticate users, but the IdP returned an error code when authenticating the user.

A target generates an HTTP error

The load balancer forwards valid HTTP responses from targets to the client, including HTTP errors. The HTTP errors generated by a target are recorded in the `HTTPCode_Target_4XX_Count` and `HTTPCode_Target_5XX_Count` metrics.

Limits for Your Application Load Balancers

To view the current limits for your Application Load Balancers, use the **Limits** page of the Amazon EC2 console or the describe-account-limits (AWS CLI) command. To request a limit increase, use the Elastic Load Balancing Limits form.

Your AWS account has the following limits related to Application Load Balancers.

Regional Limits

- Load balancers per region: 20 *
- Target groups per region: 3000

Load Balancer Limits

- Listeners per load balancer: 50
- Targets per load balancer: 1000
- Subnets per Availability Zone per load balancer: 1
- Security groups per load balancer: 5
- Rules per load balancer (not counting default rules): 100
- Certificates per load balancer (not counting default certificates): 25
- Number of times a target can be registered per load balancer: 100

Target Group Limits

- Load balancers per target group: 1
- Targets per target group: 1000

Rule Limits

- Conditions per rule: 2 (one host condition, one path condition)
- Actions per rule: 1
- Target groups per action: 1

* This limit includes both your Application Load Balancers and your Classic Load Balancers.

Document History for Application Load Balancers

The following table describes important additions to the documentation for Application Load Balancers.

- **API version:** 2015-12-01

Change	Description	Date
Authentication support	This release adds support for the load balancer to authenticate users of your applications using their corporate or social identities before routing requests. For more information, see Authenticate Users Using an Application Load Balancer.	May 30, 2018
Slow start mode	This release adds support for slow start mode, which gradually increases the share of requests the load balancer sends to a newly registered target while it warms up. For more information, see Slow Start Mode.	March 24, 2018
Resource-level permissions	This release adds support for resource-level permissions and tagging condition keys. For more information, see Authentication and Access Control in the Elastic Load Balancing User Guide.	May 10, 2018
SNI support	This release adds support for Server Name Indication (SNI). For more information, see SSL Certificates.	October 10, 2017
IP addresses as targets	This release adds support for registering IP addresses as targets. For more information, see Target Type.	August 31, 2017
Host-based routing	This release add support for routing requests based on the host names in the host header. For more information, see Host Conditions.	April 5, 2017
Security policies for TLS 1.1 and TLS 1.2	This release adds support for security policies for TLS 1.1 and TLS 1.2. For more information, see Security Policies.	February 6, 2017
IPv6 support	This release adds support for IPv6 addresses. For more information, see IP Address Type.	January 25, 2017

Change	Description	Date
Request tracing	This release adds support for request tracing. For more information, see Request Tracing for Your Application Load Balancer.	November 22, 2016
Percentiles support for the TargetResponseTime metric	This release adds support for the new percentile statistics supported by Amazon CloudWatch. For more information, see Statistics for Application Load Balancer Metrics.	November 17, 2016
New load balancer type	This release of Elastic Load Balancing introduces Application Load Balancers.	August 11, 2016

www.ingramcontent.com/pod-product-compliance
Lightning Source LLC
LaVergne TN
LVHW082041050326
832904LV00005B/259